Betty Friedan

Betty Friedan. © JP Laffont/Sygma/Corbis

Susan Oliver

Cerritos College

Betty Friedan

The Personal Is Political

THE LIBRARY OF AMERICAN BIOGRAPHY

Edited by Mark C. Carnes

New York Boston San Francisco
London Toronto Sydney Tokyo Singapore Madrid
Mexico City Munich Paris Cape Town Hong Kong Montreal

JAN 2 5 2008

Acquisitions Editor: Michael Boezi
Executive Marketing Manager: Sue Westmoreland
Editorial Assistant: Vanessa Gennarelli
Production Coordinator: Scarlett Lindsay
Project Coordination, Text Design, and Electronic Page Makeup:
  GGS Book Services
Cover Designer/Manager: John Callahan
Cover Illustration/Photo: Courtesy of Corbis
Manufacturing Buyer: Lucy Hebard
Printer and Binder: R.R. Donnelley and Sons Company,
  Harrisonburg
Cover Printer: Phoenix Color Corporation

Library of Congress Cataloging-in-Publication Data

Oliver, Susan 1945–
  Betty Friedan : the personal is political / Susan Oliver.
    p. cm.—(The library of American biography)
  Includes bibliographical references and index.
  ISBN-13: 978-0-321-39388-3 (pbk.)
  ISBN-10: 0-321-39388-0 (pbk.)
  1. Friedan, Betty. 2. Feminists—United States—Biography. I. Title.
  HQ1413.F75O45 2007
  305.42092—dc22
  [B]
                                                    2007028885

Copyright © 2008 by Pearson Education, Inc.

Please visit us at www.ablongman.com

ISBN-13: 978-0-321-39388-3
ISBN-10: 0-321-39388-0

1 2 3 4 5 6 7 8 9 10—DOH—10 09 08 07

To the young women and men of today who continue to fight the unfinished revolution for the equality, equity, and emancipation of all human beings

Contents

Editor's Preface

Some people have the curious misfortune of being overshadowed by their achievements. Harriet Beecher Stowe is an example, a remarkable writer whose *Uncle Tom's Cabin* changed the way people looked at slavery. "So you're the little woman who wrote the book that started this great war," Abraham Lincoln is reported to have said on meeting her. Stowe never escaped the powerful legacy of her most famous creation.

Betty Friedan shared a similar fate. Her *The Feminine Mystique* (1963), a mordant indictment of mid-twentieth-century domesticity, became an instant best seller. Although it did not ignite a war, it did generate the modern feminist movement. In terms of social impact, it was arguably the most important nonfiction work of the last half of the twentieth century.

But although most educated people know about Friedan's book, few know much about her life. When readers look for "Friedan" in the index to the *Oxford Companion to United States History,* for example, they are referred to *"Feminine Mystique."* Friedan's book looms so much larger than her life in part because in promoting the book, Friedan cast herself in a very small role: that of a middle-class housewife who sought only domestic contentment.

Nothing is further from the truth. From a very early age, Friedan craved notice. At Smith College she was drawn to activist causes; afterward, she worked hard as a labor journalist and threw herself into left-leaning causes. After publication of *The Feminine Mystique,* moreover, she devoted herself to a political program to ensure that women achieved equal status in American life.

Friedan, a complicated genius, carved out her own path through life; it was painful and difficult, and yet ultimately exhilarating. Susan Oliver's empathetic and sensitive biography shows not only how Friedan's personal story informed her public life, but also how her public life changed America.

On this point, Oliver speaks from personal experience. She first read *The Feminine Mystique* when she was twenty-three. At the time she had been married four years, had three young children, and had just left college. "I felt trapped," she recalled. But on reading Friedan's classic, she realized that other women had been similarly "entrapped" and, like Friedan, had found a way out. Over the next eight years, sometimes taking a single course a semester, Oliver completed her undergraduate degree at George Washington University. Her achievement, she insisted, "had been made possible by Betty Friedan." Oliver later received her Ph.D. in history from the University of California, Los Angeles. She is now a professor of history at Cerritos College in the Los Angeles area.

MARK C. CARNES

Author's Preface

Betty Friedan's impact and influence have not been not fully examined and appreciated in the current literature on women's history and women's studies. Friedan, if mentioned at all, is most often cited for writing *The Feminine Mystique* and for cofounding the National Organization for Women (NOW). Such an oversight misses her far-reaching contribution to women's rights: Betty Friedan consistently advocated that all women, no matter their martial status, their skin color, their social class, or, somewhat belatedly, their sexual orientation, are entitled to full equality and equity in American society. For her, this purpose was the unfinished revolution for women's full equality. It was the driving force of her fifty-year public life as a writer and feminist. And it is her work that has made equality and equity more of a social reality for women and men today.

Betty Friedan: The Personal Is Political makes Friedan a more visible and viable person in the history of the second wave of feminism. It is the first biography that evaluates the entirety of Friedan's life objectively through a careful and sensitive use of her writings and the works about her. Its contents demonstrate Friedan's consistent efforts to assure that women would no longer be treated as second-class citizens in American society and her understanding that to achieve equal status required changes in public policies. To illustrate the range of her activities, Friedan not only cofounded NOW in the late 1960s, but also in the last decade of her life, directed "New Paradigm: Women, Men, Work, Family, and Public Policy," a program funded by a one million dollar Ford Foundation grant. Thus, in scope and analysis, *Betty Friedan: The Personal Is Political* positions Friedan and the second-wave feminist movement within the social reform movements of the 1960s and 1970s and demonstrates how she assured that women's rights would still have a voice in the conservative backlash that began in the 1980s.

In 2002, Friedan reflected on the meaning of her life's work in the preface of a new edition of *The Feminine Mystique:* "[I]n these thirty-odd years, women breaking through the feminine mystique to their own political and economic participation and empowerment in the mainstream of society are not becoming more like men but are expressing in the public sphere some of the values that used to be expressed or allowed only in the private nurture of the home." To make her point, she continues by noting that "the mystique we had to rebel against . . . distorted [the] real values women are now embracing, with new power and zest, both in the privacy of the home and in the larger society. And in so doing they are changing the political and personal dimensions of marriage and families, home and the society they share with men." Friedan believed that as she and others "moved from consciousness to action and back again," they had developed a "new view of the personal as political and the political as personal."

Betty Friedan died on February 4, 2006, on her 85th birthday. Today historians and feminists, friends and foes, and old and young have begun assessing her legacy. The research and historical literature on Betty Friedan are robust and expanding. To keep abreast with this growing body of research and commentaries, to expand the resources on Friedan, and to support the use of this biography in college classrooms, see the Web site I have created: http://www.cerritos.edu/soliver.

SUSAN OLIVER

Acknowledgments

Writing is a solitary task; writing a book is a collaborative effort. Key people have contributed to the composition of this book. At Pearson Longman Michael Boezi, executive editor, encouraged me to submit a proposal and has been continually supportive of my work. Mark Carnes, series editor for the *Library of American Biography* series, has been pivotal by offering insightful critiques and words of encouragement at crucial times. Vanessa Gennarelli, editorial assistant, has been unflagging in her enthusiasm for the Friedan project. More significantly, she is a skilled and perceptive editor whose comments and observations have made this biography a better book. Finally, Anne Lesser and Babitha Balan added their expertise by skillfully guiding the manuscript through the production process.

I am also indebted to those who read the manuscript and offered important recommendations. These readers include: Christine Arnold-Lourie, College of Southern Maryland; Mary C. Brennan, Texas State University-San Marcos; Jacqueline M. Cavalier, Community College of Allegheny County; Jean Choate, Coastal Georgia Community College; Stephanie Cole, University of Texas at Arlington; Mary Ferrari, Radford University; Jessica Gerard, Ozarks Technical Community College; Allison J. Gough, Hawaii Pacific University; Cynthia Johnson, Cisco Junior College; Cherisse Jones-Branch, Arkansas State University; Shelly L. Lemons, St. Louis Community College at Meramec; Judy Barrett Litoff, Bryant University; Kimberly Little, University of Central Arkansas; Catherine Tobin, Central Michigan University;

Chantalle F. Verna, Florida International University; and Shirley Teresa Wajda, Kent State University.

Others who have made my job easier are Diana Carey and Laurie Ellis at the Arthur and Elizabeth Schlesinger Library on the History of Women in America. They responded positively and quickly to my requests for documents from the Betty Friedan papers, even when it meant digging through several boxes.

Closer to home, I have had the good fortune of support from the college's administrators, who gave me flexibility in my teaching schedule, and from my colleagues, whose encouraging words have meant so much. I am especially indebted to my colleague Susanna Clemans, who read the manuscript for clarity, consistency, and organization; to my friend Lois Andrews, who patiently listened to my ideas and concerns, consistently finding a silver lining behind my storm clouds; and to my children, Mark, David, and Lisa, who are my greatest cheerleaders.

But, above all, Russell Storkan, my husband, has been the greatest contributor. His good sense, incredible patience, and boundless generosity have kept me sane and happy.

Betty Friedan

1

Through a Glass Darkly

I want to fall in love and be loved and be needed by some-one. I want to have children.... [But] I know this: I don't want to marry a man and keep house for him and be the mother of his children and nothing else. I want to do something with my life—to have an absorbing interest. I want success and fame.

Bettye Goldstein, "Through a Glass Darkly," 1938

As a high school senior, Betty Friedan decided how she would live her life. Within the boundaries of cultural expectations, she wanted to be married and to have children. But she also wanted something more. She wanted to engage in an activity or profession that gave her personal fulfillment and, ideally, some public recognition. For the next 65 years, Betty Friedan never wavered from this decision because she could not: Her values, perspectives, and ambitions had already been shaped by her first 17 years.

Betty Friedan was born on February 4, 1921, at Proctor Hospital in Peoria, Illinois. Named Elizabeth (Bettye) Naomi Goldstein, she was the first child of Harry and Miriam Goldstein. Her sister, Amye, was born 18 months later, and her brother, Harry Jr., in 1926. That Bettye Goldstein spent her first seventeen and a half years in Peoria and was the daughter of

Jewish immigrants were instrumental in shaping her awareness as a child, her identity as a student, and her political activism as an adult.

Peoria, then and now, is considered the bellwether of traditional American values defined by Euro-American ancestry, religious affiliation with Protestant churches, and advocacy for the Founding Fathers' political concepts of equality and liberty. During Bettye's years in Peoria, Jewish and African American residents each comprised approximately 3 percent of the 100,000 residents of the city. As a distinctive minority, Jews living in Peoria realized that they needed to subdue or negate their cultural and religious heritage to achieve economic success and social acceptance. This factor was well understood by Bettye's father, Harry Goldstein.

Harry Goldstein (1881–1943) represents an immigrant success story. Born in a village near Kiev, he was the first of 13 children. Harry came to the United States when his parents, fearing violent actions against Jews (pogroms), decided to leave Russia. Like so many Eastern European Jews, the Goldsteins believed the United States would provide not only a safe haven from violent anti-Semitism but also be a place where they could assert their inalienable rights. Impoverished but hopeful, the family relocated to St. Louis, Missouri. In his teens, Harry decided to strike out on his own and move to Peoria. To earn money, he sold collar buttons from a peddling cart on a street corner in the city's downtown shopping area.

Goldstein's decision to move to Peoria proved wise. Peoria was Illinois's second largest city, with an expanding population and a robust and diverse economy. By his mid-twenties, Harry had saved enough money from selling collar buttons to open Goldstein's Jewelry Store in the vicinity of his peddling cart. He also married, but his wife died a few years later. (No information exists on Goldstein's first wife.) He profited from a steady and consistent clientele, and by his mid-thirties, his success was obvious: Advertisements noted that Goldstein's was the "Finest Jewelry Store in the Middle West." Bettye remembered it as the "Tiffany's of Peoria."

Bettye's mother, Miriam Leah Horwitz Goldstein (1898–1988), was the only child of Sandor and Bertha Horwitz, who, as Jews, had fled Hungary to avoid poverty and persecution. As a young man, Sandor Horwitz arrived in St. Louis in the 1880s and enrolled in medical school. In the 1890s he relocated to Peoria, established a private medical practice, and married Miriam's mother. During World War I, Dr. Horwitz served as a lieutenant colonel in the Army Medical Corps. After the war, he joined the local chapter of the American Legion, becoming one of its most avid members. Showing his genuine patriotism for America, Horwitz always proudly wore his legionnaire's cap at civic celebrations for the Fourth of July and Veteran's Day.

Miriam Horwitz, an only child, was born and educated in Peoria. Her children, as adults, and those who knew her in Peoria considered Miriam self-centered and demanding, fully aware that her petite figure, brown eyes, dark hair, and natural poise attracted attention. Miriam never lived in another city until the 1950s. In high school she expressed the desire to attend Smith College, but her parents believed that attending the two-year degree program at Peoria's Bradley College would suffice. Deeply disappointed, Miriam had no choice but to attend Bradley. After college, she was hired by the local newspaper as a writer and editor of its women's section, a job she loved.

No record exists of how Miriam Horwitz first met Harry Goldstein, but by early 1920, they had decided to marry. Miriam's parents objected to their daughter's engagement. First, Goldstein was a widower and 20 years older than she. Second, she was born in the United States and had a college degree, whereas Goldstein was born in Russia, had almost no formal education, and still spoke with a heavy accent. Strong willed, Miriam ignored her parents and married Harry Goldstein on February 3, 1920, a few days before her twenty-second birthday.

Despite his status as a first-generation immigrant, Harry Goldstein, like his wife and in-laws, placed a high value on being accepted among Peoria's upper middle class, a group that defined itself as native-born Americans who had achieved economic prosperity. He joined the reformist synagogue (Anshai Emeth Temple) and adopted the social and business practices of Peoria's prominent businessmen. Also Goldstein realized that acceptance into Peoria's upper middle class meant that his new bride must quit her job at the city's newspaper. The owner of the "best Jewelry store in Peoria" must have a wife who does not work, he told her.

As years passed, Miriam expressed resentment about how she was "forced" to quit her job. But as a new bride, she, like her husband, wanted to be accepted in the social circle of Peoria's leading citizens. Moreover, she embraced her new status: At 22, Miriam was married to an established, prosperous, and respected member of the Peoria's business community, who, in turn, gave her the potential of being featured in the society page of the local newspaper, rather than the person who did the reporting. Such a possibility must have been seductive for Miriam, a young woman already aware of her own charm and beauty and already accustomed, as an only child, to being the center of attention.

In 1924, the Goldsteins took another significant step forward in their efforts to be accepted into Peoria's upper middle class: They purchased a home in the Bluffs, the city's most prestigious neighborhood. Although the Goldsteins could not afford one of the great Victorian mansions overlooking the Illinois River Valley, they bought a comfortable brick house facing Bradley Park, a 300-acre community park with considerable open space, playgrounds, and a bandstand. Miriam furnished the house with a Steinway baby grand piano; the formal dining room had a carved-wood table that seated twelve; and the Goldsteins employed a cook, a nursemaid, and, for special occasions, a butler-chauffeur.

Freed from the mundane routine of housework, Miriam established a social presence for herself and her family and, from Bettye's vantage point, her mother did everything perfectly. Like other women of her social class, Miriam played golf and bridge, rode horseback, and swam. She participated in two Jewish women's groups and belonged to the local chapter of the Community Chest. One of her greatest pleasures was to entertain her women friends with lavish afternoon luncheons and elegant bridge parties. Proud of her good looks, Miriam spent considerable time and money sustaining her beauty. She loved to shop, used a dressmaker to tailor her suits and dresses, and considered herself one of Peoria's fashion leaders, one worthy of imitating.

Thus Harry Goldstein, a Jewish immigrant from Russia, took pride that he could purchase a home in the Bluffs, and Miriam, the daughter of Jewish immigrants from Hungary, relished being seen as one of Peoria's most accomplished and fashionable women. To make their efforts a tangible reality, the Goldsteins applied for membership in the Peoria Country Club, the most prestigious club in the city. They were rejected because the country club denied memberships to Jews as well as African Americans. This experience made Harry and Miriam Goldstein realize that they, as Jews, would remain on the fringes of Peoria's social elite.

As a young child, Bettye was oblivious to her parents' frustrations of being perceived as outsiders. Her day began at 7 A.M. That was the time that she and Amye, her sister, raced to get dressed, so they could go on walks with their father before breakfast. After supper, the family often went for car rides, along a route through the open space of Bradley Park. At the day's end, her parents listened as Bettye said her nightly prayers. First, she recited the traditional Jewish prayer, *Shema Yisrael*[*] and followed with the traditional Christian prayer, "Now I lay me down to sleep."

Much to Bettye's delight, her parents celebrated the Christmas traditions most loved by children. Bettye believed in Santa Claus, hung her stocking on the fireplace mantel, and wondered how Santa could get down the narrow chimney. She, along with her brother and sister, waited impatiently at the top of the stairs on Christmas morning until their parents gave the signal for them to run downstairs to see what Santa had brought. Her father, however, wanted to assure that his children also observed their own religious heritage by celebrating Hanukkah. For Bettye, lighting the eight candles of the Menorah was not "nearly as much fun" as Santa's visit.

---

[*]Shema Yisrael: "Hear O Israel, the Lord our God, the Lord is One." Considered as a declaration of faith, this prayer is the first prayer a Jewish child is taught.

When Bettye was an adolescent, the Goldsteins spent summer vacations at a fishing camp on Round Lake, near Hayward, Wisconsin. Harry picked this vacation spot because he enjoyed fishing, and he shared this joy with Bettye. "My father would take me fishing with him," she later wrote. "I remember the thrill, was it pike, was it bass, the sensation when a fish took the hook, and the rod bent down, and you jerked it up and began to reel in."

The Goldsteins also took their children to Chicago. Two trips represented highlights for Bettye: When she was 12, the Goldsteins went to the 1933 World's Fair, and for Bettye's 16th birthday, they treated her to a weekend that included tickets to two major stage plays, *Saint Joan* with Katharine Cornell and *Victoria Regina* with Helen Hayes.

The Goldsteins also wanted their children to have activities that taught skills and built friendships. In this effort, Bettye's mother was instrumental. She arranged for Bettye, as well as for her other children, to take lessons in golf, tennis, piano, and dancing. Bettye lacked coordination to be good at sports, which disappointed her mother. But she loved to swim, and she liked belonging to Girl Scouts and going to summer camp, where she hiked, explored nature, and took canoe trips. In addition, Bettye was pleased that her mother allowed her to make choices. For example, when she told her mother that she wanted to quit dancing lessons and take acting lessons instead, Miriam enrolled her in Mrs. Morrill's Children's Theatre. Acting lessons opened up a pathway to friendships, success, and notoriety for Bettye. She appeared in several productions of the Peoria Players, the local theater company, and acted in and directed several plays in high school. A highlight of her senior year was winning a drama award for her role as Mrs. Rochester, the madwoman in the attic, in *Jane Eyre*. It was only a two-minute walk-on where she crossed the stage emitting a hideously insane laugh, memorable for the audience and herself.

Although Bettye basked in her parents' attention as a young child, as she grew older, she became more aware of her mother's underlying unhappiness with her role as merely a wife and mother. One way that Miriam vented her frustration was to focus on the shortcomings of her children, especially her daughters. Bettye suffered most because she did not fit into what her mother considered to be the mold of a perfect child. Initially, Bettye's physical problems defined her imperfections. At birth, Bettye was so unhealthy that the doctors and her parents believed she would not live long. She had weak lungs, which meant she battled bronchitis each winter as a child and asthma for all the years that followed, and she had bowed legs, which meant she had to wear iron braces for her first three years. Replacing the leg braces were braces for her teeth, and at age 11, Bettye needed thick-lens glasses because she was almost blind in one eye. Miriam was most disappointed that Bettye had not inherited her beauty. Even though she had her mother's large brown deep-lidded eyes, Bettye had the "misfortune" of inheriting her father's long, prominent Jewish nose.

In addition, Bettye's personal habits increased her mother's aggravation. She paid no attention to the way she dressed, quite opposite from her mother's attentive grooming, and she refused to keep her bedroom clean, a room she shared with her sister Amye. Strong willed and intolerant of frustrations, she was prone to angry outbursts that rattled windows. She threw a book so hard at her sister that Amye needed stitches; another time she hit a boy on the head with a hoe; and yet another time, she tore a patch of hair from the head of her best friend. As an adolescent, Bettye began to feel an overwhelming sense of inadequacy as a consequence of her mother's relentless expressions of disappointment. At that point, she began to realize that she, unlike her mother, sister, and friends, had not been "well endowed physically, neither with health nor beauty."

Bettye's experiences with her father were dramatically different. He was, as she later wrote, the "texture, the heart, and the center" of her early understanding of herself. As a child, she missed him when his work meant he would not be home for dinner or had to miss some days of their family vacations. In her later writing, she often referred to father as "Daddy." The underlying reason for Bettye's positive experiences was because Harry Goldstein favored her over his other children. Like him, she was exceedingly bright and inquisitive, the qualities that made Bettye an intellectual companion. With great pride, Goldstein showed friends and customers her essays and poems and bragged about Bettye's accomplishments in school. More significantly, he saved all her essays and poems, each a "master-piece," by putting them in his safe.

The most obvious display of his favoritism happened at the dinner table when Harry Goldstein introduced topics on current events or interesting ideas that he had read about. Topics ranged from Lindbergh's successful transatlantic flight to Paris in 1928 to the ravages of Hitler against Jews and communists in the 1930s. Goldstein created this dinner-table environment so his children would not only learn about the world beyond their own self-interests but also to teach them to express their opinions. The impact on Bettye was positive. In these conversations, she was the one asked about the political issues of the day and the one who could instantly solve a math problem he might pose.

Moreover, discussions at dinner were central to the Goldsteins' objective to shape their children's perspectives on social justice. In the 1936 presidential election, Harry Goldstein told his children that he and their mother had voted for Franklin Roosevelt because his New Deal policies were trying to help people in need, and during the height of the Great Depression, the Goldsteins had their children prepare Christmas baskets of toys and food for poor families living in Peoria.

An equal positive force in Bettye's life was school. She started first grade at Whittier School, a few blocks from her home, in the fall of 1927. Immediately, she felt important because she always had the right answers. It also quickly became apparent to her teacher and parents that she was much brighter than her classmates. Learning this, her mother had her IQ (intelligence quotient) measured. With a score of 180, Bettye was labeled an "exceptional genius," which allowed her to skip a grade while at Whittier.

Thinking back on her childhood, Betty Friedan stated that learning to read was one of the greatest benefits of her grammar school education because books satisfied her insatiable intellectual curiosity. In grade school, her friends nicknamed her "book-worm." Often she read one or two books a day, typically checking out the maximum number of books from the city's public library; she also happily anticipated her birthday and Christmas because her gifts were most often books. Bettye's parents became worried, however, that she spent so much time reading, and they were equally concerned about frequent temper tantrums. To understand their daughter better, the Goldsteins had Bettye examined by a psychologist, who, after testing her, advised the Goldsteins to "leave the brilliant girl to her own devices."

Although gaining the right to be left to her "own devices" as a learner, Bettye's true happiness in school came from having a close-knit group of friends. Starting in the second grade and extending through junior high, Bettye's friends, who also lived in the Bluffs, were the daughters and sons of Peoria's leading citizens. These were the friends that took the same lessons in golf and tennis, belonged to the same Girl Scout troop, and went to the same summer camp. But her happiest times were when she and her friends had the free time to create an imaginative world of games and secret clubs. For these, Bettye became the group's ringleader.

At first, Bettye and her friends played "let's pretend" games such as "dress-up" and "mystery." By the sixth grade, the group decided that forming secret clubs would be more fun. Their first was the Baddy, Baddy Club whose purpose was to create classroom incidents that stirred up excitement and maddened teachers. Members would decide on some type of action, and, when signaled by Bettye, they would create an uproar: They dropped books or erupted into coughing fits when the teacher or other students were making presentations, and they refused to be monitors. When the club was banned by Mr. Murphy, the school principal, the group retaliated by forming a new club, the Gummy, Gummy Club. Its purpose was to protest by chewing large wads of gum during class. In response to this second club, Mr. Murphy called the rebels to his office, threatening to expel them if they continued with their actions. More significantly, he advised Bettye and her friends that they had great talent for leadership—but they "must use it for good, not evil." Bettye Goldstein took his advice, a decision that served others well.

Bettye's social clique continued when they went to Roosevelt Junior High School, but basketball games, school dances, and

Saturday night parties replaced secret clubs. She also worked on *The Reflector*, the school's newspaper, and discovered that she loved seeing her words and byline in print. Bettye's first eight years in school increased her confidence because she proved that she was not, as her mother claimed, messy, clumsy, inadequate, bad, naughty, or ugly. Instead she felt sheer delight because she easily mastered Latin, French, algebra, and geometry. More especially, Bettye was happy because she had close friends.

But this happiness ended when Bettye and her friends began Central High School. The binding glue of their social clique began to dissolve, causing Bettye to conclude that she had dropped out of her friends' world.

Several reasons account for Bettye's sense of abandonment. When she started, Central High had a two-shift schedule to avoid overcrowding. She was placed in the afternoon shift, whereas her friends were in the morning shift. Also, because Bettye skipped a grade in grammar school, she was younger than her friends. When her girlfriends began to blossom as young ladies, she found herself still in a little girl's body. That, along with the fact that she wore thick-lens glasses and had the "Goldstein" nose, made her not only physically immature but less attractive. Finally, there was prejudice: Bettye, unlike most of her friends, was not asked to join a sorority because the school's sororities (and fraternities) excluded Jews. It was the rejection of not being asked to join a sorority because she was a Jew that hurt Bettye the most.

Although high school sororities and fraternities were not sanctioned by Peoria's school administration, three of each existed "unofficially" at Central High School. Members of these unofficial clubs controlled the social life at the school. This meant that Bettye, accustomed to being the ringleader of the social activities for the past eight years, was now excluded from the high school version of secret clubs. By the end of her freshman year, Bettye saw herself as a social outcast, and during her sophomore year, she became convinced that all her friends no longer liked her.

Added to her social problems at school were problems at home where her parents often argued about money. The impact of the Great Depression dramatically diminished the profits of Goldstein's Jewelry Store. Despite limited earnings, Harry Goldstein refused to fire his employees because he did not want them to join the bread lines of the unemployed. Less profit meant that Miriam no longer had a generous allowance to employ servants, spend on parties, and purchase the latest fashions. Angry with her husband, Miriam retaliated by buying what she wanted on credit, hiding the bills, and compounding the debt by gambling secretly and unsuccessfully.

Absence of money often transformed the evening dinner table from one of lively debates into a battlefield in which Bettye and her siblings, innocent bystanders, suffered as much as the adversaries. When provoked by Miriam, Harry Goldstein's face would redden, he would bang his fist down on the table, and then rise and storm out of the room. In response, Miriam made allies of her children. In their presence, she ridiculed her husband for his accent and lack of education, qualities that, in her eyes, proved him not only less equal to her but also unable to assimilate into the social and business community of Peoria. She also lured her children into a conspiracy against their father, beseeching them to keep quiet about the purchases she made for them, for herself, or for the house.

Bettye tried various ways to deal emotionally with her parents' battles. She often found herself part of her mother's conspiracy. Yet, at times, she sided with her father, who was her intellectual companion. She empathized with her father but longed for her mother's love. These conflicting emotions gave her an unbearable sense of feeling bad, deep inside herself. To cope, she vowed, at age 15, never to allow her parents to make her cry again. Thereafter, when the shouting began, she walled herself in to protect herself from the pain of her parents' battles.

These were, indeed, dark times. Although she had found a way to cope with her problems at home, Bettye had a harder time accepting that she was not popular with boys and was not asked to join a high school sorority. In her autobiographical essay "Through a Glass Darkly," she reveals that she "shed buckets of tears," hated Peoria, and believed she would never marry because she lacked sex appeal. Mourning her loss of friends, Bettye spent late afternoons at the cemetery near her house, sitting on a gravestone and reading poems by Emily Dickinson. On weekend nights, she looked out of her bedroom window, thinking about how her friends were having a good time. At these darkest of times Bettye tried to make sense out of her new social nonstatus. Had she been rejected by a sorority because she was too smart and not pretty? Or was it because she was Jewish?

Bettye was bewildered. Up to this time her brains and looks had not kept her from being part of the "in crowd" at school. She also could not understand why her Jewishness now mattered. She, like her parents, had assimilated. She had never gone to a Jewish summer camp and had participated in the socially accepted activities and clubs. Therefore, she assumed that her religious and cultural heritage did not impact her popularity and friendships. Rejection by the sorority shattered this understanding of her social world. For answers, she turned to her parents.

Miriam responded by pointing out to Bettye that her inattentiveness to her personal appearance, her "Jewish" nose, her temper, and her inclination to "show off" her intellectual abilities might well be the reasons she was no longer popular. As an adult, Friedan quipped that her mother's assessment caused her to see herself in high school as an "ugly duckling, a freak with brains." At the time, however, Bettye felt even worse because, it seemed, her mother blamed her for not being in a sorority.

By contrast, Harry dealt with his daughter's rejection by sharing his experiences of anti-Semitism. Unlike his wife, he could not disguise his accent and Jewish nose. He also told his daughter about his painful experiences of discrimination: Though respected by businessmen in Peoria, he had learned that respect was not the same as friendship. His social interactions with these men ended when the store closed; after six o'clock his daytime friends simply would not talk with him. More importantly, Harry Goldstein conveyed to his daughter his own dreams that he, as an impoverished first-generation Jewish immigrant from Eastern Europe, had not been able to realize. One unrealized dream was his inability to finish school, a legacy he refused to pass onto Bettye.

As an adolescent, Bettye drew on her painful experience of discrimination as a starting point to understand herself better. As an adult, she remembered this rejection and made this experience the starting point for an agenda for social reform. "When you're a Jewish girl growing up on the right side of the tracks in the Midwest you're marginal," she told an interviewer. "You're IN but you're not and you grow up an observer." When rejected by the sorority, Bettye became that observer, one who then saw that Jews, just because of their religious and cultural heritage, were pushed to the margins of social acceptance in Peoria. From this vantage point, she began to realize that people of color, just because of genetics, and women, just because of chromosome structure, suffered the same fate.

As a teenager, however, Bettye dealt differently with her experience. Unintentionally, the responses from her parents provided the necessary tools to restructure her social life at Central High School. Angered by her mother's reminders of her inadequacies, she decided to build on her strengths as a thinker, writer, and organizer. Comforted by her father's admissions of discrimination, she began to come to terms with the unspoken, but nonetheless real, existence of anti-Semitism in Peoria. From her anger and new awareness, Bettye Goldstein vowed that her friends from the past, as well as any in the present or future, might not like her, but they would learn to respect her. Bettye Goldstein had rebounded.

Bettye began her junior year with a whole new outlook. She understood that there were two ways to gain recognition in high school—either to be very popular or to be very prominent and successful in activities. Knowing that her absence of good looks and her abundance of brains meant she would never be popular, she decided to make her mark by participating in school activities. She also changed her approach to friendships. Instead of relying on only one or two close friends within a tight social clique, she decided to have many good friends whose interests and activities were as diverse as hers.

The activity that gave Bettye her greatest reward was writing for student publications. It was here that she gained notoriety, friendships, and increased self-confidence. In her junior and senior years, Bettye wrote for the high school newspaper, the *Opinion*. She began by writing book reviews, then moved onto writing "Cabbage and Kings," a weekly column that typically poked fun at social issues at the school. In retrospect, Bettye's work on the school newspaper, though intrinsically rewarding, was a stepping-stone for her most rewarding venture—one that made her senior year the "most perfect year."

The venture was publishing *Tide*, the school's first literary magazine that had the added distinction of being independent of the school's curriculum, clubs, and financial underwriting. At first, a student-generated literary magazine seemed only a hazy dream, a recurring one that Bettye had had since the summer before her senior year. She mentioned this dream to four friends who also worked on student publications; one of these was Doug Palmer, who became a lifelong friend. At first, Bettye and the others had a hard time fathoming how to pay for printing the magazine, and they were unsure if they could find time in their busy schedules for such an ambitious project. But Bettye's dream was tempting, seducing them to find solutions for practical problems. By asking questions, they discovered that the *Peoria Journal-Transcript*, the city's local newspaper, would print sufficient copies of their magazine for $50 per issue. Second, at the suggestion of Bettye's father, they learned that they could cover the costs of printing by soliciting donations from local merchants.

Once the practical problems had solutions, the burgeoning journalists began to map out the design and content for their literary magazine. They decided that *Tide* would be the same size as the *Reader's Digest,* and each issue would be 16 pages long and include stories, poems, and essays. Although they solicited articles from students, they wrote most of the copy themselves. They also did all the editing, layout, and proofreading. To promote their literary magazine, they advertised, spoke at school assemblies, and had a radio program. And they shared the responsibility of selling copies, each priced at 10 cents. In their senior year, Bettye and her friends published three issues of *Tide* (November 1937, March 1938, and May 1938).

Bettye considered that publishing *Tide* was the "biggest thing" in her life as a senior. It was the first time that she had taken an idea and made it, along with friends, into a concrete reality. Bettye captures her infectious enthusiasm in her senior year autobiographical essay. She tells how much she enjoyed collaborating with friends who shared her passion for writing, ideas, and challenging the status quo. Although *Tide* meant "hours of fear and worry and wishing there had never been an idea of a magazine," their hard work led to "days of exaltation—and finally a success beyond all dreams." With great gusto, she tells about how she and Doug Palmer "trembled in their boots" when they took the copy of the first issue to be typeset at the city's newspaper. Next she reveals their pride that, after reading the page proofs, they could see that *Tide* looked even better than they could have ever imagined. When their first issue came out in November, the friends realized that their dream had really come true: It was, for Bettye, "a perfect moment."

Bettye graduated from Central High School on June 9, 1938. Likely, while waiting to be called to receive her diploma, she recounted her successes in her final two years. She had made new friends, written book reviews and two columns for the school newspaper, and started *Tide*. In addition she had belonged to a long list of academic and social clubs; gained honors for her writing, acting, and grades; and spent summers working for the city's newspaper, a settlement house, and tutoring German émigrés in English. She ended these remarkable years as one of six valedictorians and had been accepted to a long and prestigious list of colleges. Bettye had the choice to attend either the University of Chicago or Stanford University, or she could choose among the prestigious women's colleges of Vassar, Radcliffe College, Wellesley, or Smith. She decided on Smith College, located in Northampton, Massachusetts. No doubt, her mother, whose own dream to attend Smith had never been realized, had much to do with her decision. Most certainly, her father was grateful that his daughter would achieve a dream that had not been possible for him. Bettye was reassured because she could now leave Peoria, a place that she now saw as unfair and unjust, and relocate to the East Coast, where she could broaden her horizons.

As she waited to receive her diploma on graduation day, she may well have recalled the final words in her autobiographical essay: "[T]he past seventeen years," she wrote, "have been a succession of striving for something, and thinking once I would achieve it I would be content, and then achieving it—and not being content but striving for something else." When her name was called, Bettye Naomi Goldstein walked across the stage to receive her high school diploma, knowing that she would always strive for new challenges and adventures. The first of these would be exploring the life of her mind at Smith College.

2

Exploring the Life of the Mind

At Smith, [it] was your responsibility to take a stand on political issues, to figure out where you stood, personally, on religion and politics, no matter what the faith or politics of your mother or father; and what you did or would do with your life would, could, must make a difference. We were not, then, given a clear sense of career possibilities at Smith, but a lot of us got a wonderfully clear, inescapable social conscience, an inescapable sense of political responsibility.

Betty Friedan, *Life So Far*, 2000

Bettye Goldstein arrived at Smith College in late September, a few days after the so-called great hurricane of 1938 stormed the campus with its winds of 115 miles per hour. Perhaps the hurricane helped condition the campus community for the arrival of a young woman who also stormed the campus with her intellect, activism, and commitment to fight against injustice. Much like her final two years in high school, Bettye made her mark at Smith College by drawing on her talent as a writer, her ambition to excel, and her advocacy for social justice.

Established in 1871, Smith College was committed to assuring that its students were given the same rigorous education as offered by the all-male (at that time) Ivy League colleges of

Harvard, Yale, and Princeton. Fundamental to meeting its objective, Smith College offered a classical liberal arts education and recruited scholars with exceptional credentials. In 1940, 14 percent of the present or former members of the faculty had recently received Guggenheim Fellowships; 63 percent of the college's professors were women; and, unlike other prestigious private colleges, the faculty included a considerable number of Jews who were on the cutting edge of their academic expertise.

William Allan Neilson, the college president from 1917 to 1939, was responsible, in large part, for the exceptional quality of the Smith College faculty. A tireless advocate for progressive education and social justice, Neilson attracted scholars to Smith who shared his perspective. During Bettye's years there, Reinhold Niebuhr, advocate of Christian socialism, and Eleanor Roosevelt, advocate for social welfare, were among those invited to speak at campus-wide meetings. In the classroom and in public forums, Bettye was continually exposed to strongly liberal, antifascist positions, and values promoted in these settings were free speech, tolerance, progress, social responsibility, social justice, community, democracy, and peace.

By contrast, the social milieu of the college sustained socially conservative, elitist attitudes, which were not all that different from those in Peoria. Most obvious was the absence of diversity in its student body of 2,000 young women. Most of them were Euro-American, from middle- to upper-class households, and worshipped at Protestant churches. Roman Catholics and Jews each comprised less than twenty women at the college, and the handful of African American students were light skinned and from prominent families. Like Bettye's parents, most fathers were businessmen, bankers, or professionals, and most mothers were homemakers, who filled their time as volunteers in civic and church organizations.

Of more immediate import for Bettye, Smith College created a lifestyle for its students that resembled the homes they had left behind. Rather than dormitory living, students were assigned to large older homes on campus that had been remodeled to accommodate fifty to seventy students. All residential houses included a housemother, to help students with problems and oversee their behaviors, and maids, to make beds, clean bathrooms, and serve dinner. In these large spacious residential houses, students could invite friends or faculty to afternoon tea, form study groups, and play bridge. Bettye was assigned to Chapin House and was delighted to discover that Natalie Turlow, her roommate, was also Jewish.

Perhaps the fact that she and Natalie were part of a very small minority of students prompted Bettye to reflect on how she, a Jewish girl from the Midwest, might fit in at Smith College. Drawing from experiences in Peoria, Bettye realized she had two choices. To help assure that she would have friends and gain acceptance, she could mute her Jewishness. Or she could embrace it, with the risk that she would be ignored and disliked. Unshackled from the family and community expectations of Peoria, Bettye decided to make her Jewish linage and heritage integral to her self-image and actions. This commitment was tested two months into her first year: She was asked by college president Neilson to support his efforts to increase immigration quotas for Jews trying to escape from Nazi Germany, which was a highly unpopular political stance at Smith College as well as in the United States.

Students at the college were required to attend weekly assemblies. Often Neilson used these meetings to remind students that they, as individuals, were part of a larger world community, and as members, they needed to support causes of social justice. In the student-faculty convocation of mid-November 1938, Neilson's reminder was far from gentle: He urged students to sign a petition that demanded President Franklin Roosevelt and Congress relax immigration quotas to give asylum to Jewish refugees trying to escape Nazi Germany. Thus far, the federal government had resisted pressure to relax immigration quotas for Jews because it did not want to add more workers to the labor pool during the Great Depression. This petition also stated that Smith College would actively recruit new students from the émigrés. Because Hitler's hatred for Jews was so fierce and cruel, Neilson reasoned, citizens of America, as believers in freedom, needed to remember their commitment to a common humanity. By doing so, Neilson challenged students not only to affirm their common humanity with Jews living in Germany and Eastern Europe, but also to confront the reality publicly that continued strict immigration quotas were an example of American anti-Semitism.

After the campus meeting, the women in Chapin House discussed President Neilson's request. Bettye was surprised by the conversation. Many students made clear that they were against the petition because they did not want any more Jews at Smith. Also, the greatest advocates for signing the petition were three Protestants. By contrast, four residents, wealthy Jews from Cincinnati, remained silent, and their silence resounded in Bettye's ears.

Bettye took up Neilson's call and asked others to sign the petition. Because no consensus was reached at the house meeting, the residents decided to leave the petition on a hall table to allow for additional signatures. A small group from Chapin signed, Bettye among them. Absent were signatures from the four Jewish girls from Cincinnati. The fate of the petition in Chapin Hall was consistent with its fate among the general student body—President Neilson's petition failed. That students of Smith College rejected the petition reflected the mood of most Americans in 1938. That year *Fortune* magazine surveyed its readers, asking them whether they would support raising immigration quotas so more Jews could gain visas. Two-thirds of the respondents stated they wanted "to keep Jews out" of the United States.

The combination of Neilson's plea and the absence of signatures on the petition at Chapin House helped Bettye understand that American anti-Semitism had larger consequences than rejection to social clubs. She realized that Jews who wanted to be accepted were capable of being just as anti-Semitic as non-Jews. Moreover, the fate of Neilson's request demonstrated that American anti-Semitism was more powerful than advocacy for human rights.

On a personal level, Bettye's decision to support the petition marked greater self-confidence because she was forced to confront conflicting values and emotions. On one hand, she very much wanted to fit in, to be popular. On the other, she felt compelled to act on her advocacy for social justice. By supporting the petition, Bettye Goldstein decided that it was far more important to act on her personal values than mimic the attitudes of others. Taking the risk to be honest led to a new discovery: Bettye was liked for who she was. As a freshman, she bonded with others who relished learning. She discovered that she was no longer seen as a freak for having brains and excluded by the Protestant and Catholic girls because she was Jewish. Such acceptance, as she later wrote, made her "sparkle with the joy and bliss of knowing" she belonged.

Having a better sense of herself enabled Bettye to take full advantage of the vibrant texture of Smith College. In music history she listened to Beethoven, Mozart, and Debussy and brought away a lifelong love for classical music. Literature courses exposed her to books about rites of passage. Reading Virginia Wolfe, Thomas Mann, James Joyce, and Leo Tolstoy helped her better understand her emotional makeup, and it also provided a context for her growing awareness of political issues. After reading Flaubert's *Madame Bovary*, she wondered if its theme helped explain her mother. Hemingway's *For Whom the Bell Tolls* exposed her to the political issues of the Spanish Civil War (1936), and John Reed's *Ten Days That Shook the World* revealed the Russian Revolution from the perspective of the communists.

The richness of a classical liberal arts education enticed Bettye. Yet what captivated her were the classes in Pearce Hall, the location of the psychology department. As a high school senior, she had expressed interest in majoring in psychology because she wanted to understand her feelings of inferiority and the conflicts with her parents. These personal issues prompted her to register for Psychology II in her freshman year. This course ranked as one of her favorites that year because it required students to test patterns of human behavior through a hands-on process of conducting experiments using the scientific method.

Learning that the scientific method can be used to test factors that influence human behavior gave Bettye the intellectual tools to examine existing social structures. Her first opportunity to apply these tools came when she took a course in social psychology from James Gibson in her sophomore year. As an avowed radical, Gibson believed that Marxist socialism provided the only theory for social action for workers, and, as a political activist, he supported workers' rights and battled against fascism. In lectures, Gibson made clear that socialism offered better solutions to economic and social inequalities than capitalism; and in assignments, he challenged students to critique the assumptions of mainstream American society. One such assignment required students to read and assess *Middletown* (1929), the sociological study conducted by Robert and Helen Lynd that delineated the social norms of middle-class citizens in Muncie, Indiana.

Bettye understood and responded to Gibson's objective in assigning *Middletown* as an example of what was wrong with American society. More significantly, she made meaningful connections between the study and her own experiences growing up in another typical midwestern town. After reading the Lynds's study, she realized her miserable experiences in Peoria were not personal. Instead, like Muncie, these experiences reflected the social norms of Peoria dictated specific expectations of behaviors for its residents. Bettye also realized that these expectations had a direct impact on her mother. Both her mother and the middle-class women of Muncie believed their role as wives and mothers represented the socially sanctioned goals of female existence. Thus these women were expected to gain total fulfillment in their domestic role that Bettye knew was not true for her mother.

As a junior, Bettye enrolled in two courses that would be pivotal in shaping her emerging political perspective. The first of these was an economics course taught by Dorothy Wolff Douglas, a political radical and feminist. Douglas's course exposed Bettye to a Marxist critique of capitalism. Two themes—the role of the working class in bringing about revolutionary change and the role of women as second-class citizens—made the greatest impression on Bettye. She listened as Douglas detailed the ways that capitalism oppressed workers, echoing many of the same issues and themes first presented in Gibson's course in social psychology.

More significant, Douglas exposed Bettye to a feminist interpretation of political culture. As part of the economics course, Douglas made the comparison of attitudes toward women's expected roles in Nazi Germany and in the Soviet Union. Bettye took careful notes as Douglas explained that the Nazi ideology of *Kinder, Küche, und Kirche* (children, kitchen, and church) placed children at the center of family lives, celebrated motherhood, and opposed women working outside the home in professional positions. As an ideology, it argued that women should ignore any aspirations of an intellectual or professional life because they are more naturally suited for domestic responsibilities. In citing this example, Douglas told students she was not only against the fascist approach to separate spheres but also that she believed women in the United States were subjected to similar pressures. To illustrate that women had alternatives, Douglas offered the example of women living in the Soviet Union, where socialist principles gave women equality of opportunity, with matching wages, and, in some cases, earnings exceeding those of men. Persuaded by Douglas's ideas, Bettye applied these perspectives in assigned essays and articles for student publications.

Bettye also enrolled in Eric Koffka's course in Gestalt psychology in her junior year. Koffka, one of the founders of Gestalt, had emigrated from Germany in 1924 and spent most of his American career at Smith. Gestalt theory, according to Koffka, assumes that a human being is an ever-changing open system who interacts with his or her environment. Thus a person acquires "true knowledge" by continuously interpreting experiences and then using this knowledge to make positive changes within his or her larger social structure.

As a student, Bettye embraced Koffka's Gestalt theory: She liked its focus on large questions, its avoidance of narrow specialization, and its requirement to question value systems. For a young woman engaged in her own journey to gain greater self-confidence, a theory that emphasized reinterpreting experiences and making positive changes must have had great appeal. Equally, the implication of Gestalt theory—that societies can change for the better—gave Bettye an intellectual framework to argue for reform. Years later, Betty Friedan often claimed that her exposure to Eric Koffka and Gestalt theory had the greatest influence on her education.

In addition to her studies, Bettye Goldstein pursued her interest as a journalist. As a sophomore, she revived a student-sponsored magazine, *Smith College Monthly* (*SCM*). She transformed the monthly literary magazine into one that published articles on social and political issues. For the next three years, she contributed articles and served as the magazine's managing editor. By her sophomore year, Bettye was also on the staff of the school newspaper, the *Smith College Associated News* (*SCAN*). As a junior, she was its news editor, and as a senior, the editor in chief. In a position to control content, Bettye made both publications a bully pulpit that advocated the agenda of left-leaning liberals and radicals: workers' rights, academic freedom, antifascism, and, until Pearl Harbor, nonintervention in World War II.

In her last two years at Smith College, Bettye became known among her peers and faculty members as an influential, compelling, and controversial figure on campus, a reputation she earned by both her academic performance and her work on student publications. As a junior and senior, she discovered ways to channel her ingrained passion for social justice into public advocacy for political causes. For her, fighting injustice meant direct action: It was a personal, moral, and religious responsibility. As a student and journalist, she challenged herself to figure out where she stood on religion and politics and to take a stand, even if it meant rejecting the values of her parents and social class.

Instrumental in shaping Bettye's political perspective was her exposure to and participation in the student activist movement of the 1930s and early 1940s. Cited by historians as the most effective radical organization in the history of American student politics, this movement began in the mid-1930s as students faced the two crises of their generation: the ravages of the Great Depression and the specter of a second world war. Seeking fundamental change in America's economic and social policies, students in this movement were a diverse coalition of communists, socialists, liberals, and pacifists. From college campuses to national meetings in Washington, D.C., from the classrooms to summer workshops, the student movement challenged young people such as Bettye Goldstein to reexamine the bourgeois (middle-class) culture of their parents, to identify with the working class, and to make racial and ethnic diversity a priority. Like so many young adults, Bettye gravitated to the American student movement because, as political scientist and former 1930s student activist John P. Roche recalled, it offered them the opportunity to transform the United States from a "nation sunk in poverty and depression, racked by racial and religious discrimination and seemingly on the 'The Road to War'. . . to a society governed by the principles of economic and political justice and human equality, living in a peaceful world."

Student activists challenged the Roosevelt administration. They demanded that New Deal policies be expanded to include people in poverty and minority groups who suffered racial discrimination, and they called for a pacifist foreign policy that opposed fascism but, at the same time, kept the United States out of the Second World War. For those in the student movement, these two positions were connected: To be a belligerent in World War II would threaten civil liberties and derail any policies that might end poverty and racial discrimination. These objectives were also personal: Student activists realized that their generation would fight that war. Bettye was swept up with the ideals in the student movement, but her pacifist stance ended when the Japanese bombed American ships at Pearl Harbor on December 7, 1941, "a day," noted Franklin Roosevelt, "that will live in infamy."

Before Pearl Harbor, Bettye made her political perspective the bedrock of her work as a writer and editor of student publications. In the fall of 1940, she organized the content of the *Smith College Monthly (SCM)* around a current campus debate among faculty and students on the issue of whether to disallow statements of dissent against America's increased interventionist policies in World War II—that is, to curb academic freedom and free speech. Bettye marshaled her forces to disagree. As editor of *SCM*, she solicited articles from faculty, administrators, and students that defended freedom of speech during wartime. In her article, she argued that when the words *defense, civilization,* and *democracy* are used as a rationale to curtail free speech, Americans who support these limitations have lost sight of what these principles mean. Bettye also used her editorial power to argue the radical agenda of the student movement in the college newspaper, *Smith College Associated News (SCAN)*. As news editor and then as editor in chief, she argued for the rights of workers to use labor strikes to pressure for higher wages and for guarantees that free speech and academic freedom would be sustained at Smith College.

In February 1941, Bettye, as the editor of *SCAN*, decided to report on a two-day meeting of students in Washington, D.C. Sponsored by the American Youth Congress, an umbrella organization of student activist groups, the meeting was organized to oppose the Lend Lease Act, which would help the British war effort. The main event was a march from Capitol Hill to the White House. In that protest march, 2,000 young people, whose backgrounds ranged from students of elite colleges to sharecroppers from the South, marched down Pennsylvania Avenue, chanting, "Johnny Wants a Job, Not a Gun." Their chant, a reconfiguration of Dalton Trumbo's title, *Johnny Got His Gun* (1939), made clear that they feared economic support for Great Britain would not only lead to American involvement in another world war but also would derail social legislation for the poor and erode civil liberties and workers' rights in the United States.

The day of the march Bettye arrived early and secured a place in the front row along the parade route, so she could accurately report the event for the college newspaper. The protest march started peacefully. But soon she realized that policemen on horses were riding along the sidewalk toward the marching students. Their intent was to stop the protest. To get out of the way, Bettye stepped off the curb and was pushed into the crowd of marchers. Next, she found herself marching with the protesters and perhaps even chanting their mantra, "Johnny Wants a Job, Not a Gun." And she liked how it felt. "I wasn't just an observer, a writer," she later wrote in her memoir *Life So Far*. On that cold day in February 1941, Bettye Goldstein marched because she believed in its cause.

Clearly, Bettye, now in editorial control of two student publications, had become a passionate writer and actor in the political arena of politics. She relished how her position went against the grain of the status quo. Her opposition was borne out of her own sense of empowerment. Bettye took positions that were clearly against the tide of the campus culture because she believed she must work for a better society and seek truth. She had become, as Marcia Cohen has written, "the throaty social conscience, who argued, always, for justice, for the poor, for the disadvantaged."

As a burgeoning political activist, Bettye wanted to learn and experience more about the issues, causes, and actions of left-leaning liberal and radical groups. This desire motivated her to apply for a summer workshop at the Highlander Folk School (HFS). Founded in 1932 near the small Cumberland Plateau town of Monteagle, Tennessee, HFS was an adult training and education center designed to develop leadership and organizational structures among economically and socially oppressed southerners. From their experiences at HFS, participants would have the tools to create a new social order that assured social and economic justice and respect for all individuals, irrespective of social class, gender, or skin color. The focus of workshops and activities of HFS in the 1930s was to expose and train southern workers in strategies of political and union organization for the nascent southern labor movement, not an easy task.

The summer residence program, which included about twenty people, had two sequential workshops. The first was a two-week writers' workshop that focused on exploring methods that made the documentary writing style informative and interesting. In her own writing assignment for the workshop, Bettye expresses wonderment about being part of such a diverse group of writers. Participants in this writer's workshop included a novelist from Cincinnati, a Chinese medical student enrolled at Johns Hopkins, a primary school principal from Georgia, a woman who ran for governor of Tennessee, a minister from Kentucky, a "hack writer" from New York, an 18-year-old girl from Kentucky who had won a magazine prize for a story, and a federal relief administrator from Chicago. She liked the group's cooperative work, the give-and-take that happened when they did their daily chores as well as the overall sense that everyone was part of a larger community. The requirement for admission was the desire to write, not the ability to pay the tuition, a fact that was striking to Bettye. One woman in her workshop, for example, paid her fee with a hickory-smoked ham, some blackberry jam, and a great cake, chocolate and white with a jelly filling and coconut.

In the second workshop, Bettye took part in a four-week program designed to educate participants about unions, workers, and the economy and to provide practical information on how to conduct union business on the picket line and at rallies. Most participants were labor activists. Although she never applied the tactics and strategies presented in this workshop as a union organizer, Bettye did gain a greater understanding of the tensions between the middle class and working class. She responded by reconsidering her middle-class background in an article she wrote for the Highlander newsletter in the fall of 1941. In this article, Bettye admits that she had no exposure to the working-class families of Peoria because she, among the 1 percent of the population, lived on the "Bluffs," whereas the working class lived at the "lower end" of Peoria. She also reveals that she learned about the capitalist ethic by listening to her father's friends. Reconsidering their comments, Bettye points out that these businessmen agreed that workers were greedy if they demanded higher wages or joined labor unions. But from her internship at Highlander Folk School, Bettye now realized that the businessmen were the greedy ones because they valued their profits more than the quality of life of their workers.

Beyond what she wrote, Bettye's time at Highlander Folk School introduced her to the ideas, concerns, and agenda of the working class. Without that six-week internship, she could have comprehended these issues intellectually, but she would have not understood the emotional context. She met and worked with southerners committed to political activism, knowing they could well encounter exclusion, failure, and violence. She befriended the staff members of the school, individuals committed to radical political change. In these individuals, she had found a group of like-minded political activists. Over the next few years, Bettye continued to exchange letters with key staff members of HFS. Her letters told of her challenges as a journalist and editor of student publications because she, like them, argued the unpopular positions of supporting workers and labor unions and of opposing U.S. economic and military intervention in World War II.

Emboldened by the internship at HFS, Bettye returned to Smith College for her final year. She completed her degree requirements in psychology and wrote her senior honor's thesis. Bettye's last semester at Smith College was her most challenging because she had come to grips with her future—one that could mean marriage, a career in journalism, or graduate school. This challenge made her uncomfortable because she was unsure about what she wanted. As she sifted through her options, Bettye decided that she would not move back to Peoria, and she would not get married because she had neither an engagement ring nor a serious boyfriend. Next she took a hard look at the prospect of pursuing a career as a journalist for a major national magazine. This, too, was not an option because she, like other women, would be hired as a researcher with almost no hope of being promoted to a reporter or editor. Such subordination, for her, would be unacceptable.

That left Bettye with the obvious choice: graduate school. Intellectually, she had been inspired by her courses in psychology; personally, she had been gratified by her achievements at Smith College. She had received the Arthur Ellis Hamm Scholarship as a freshman, become a member of Phi Beta Kappa as a sophomore, was elected to Sigma XI, a national honor society for the sciences, as a senior, and would graduate *summa cum laude* (with highest honors). Graduate school might lead to becoming a professor, someone who could be as inspiring and influential as Dorothy Douglas. Graduate school also represented the first step to becoming a psychiatrist, an ambition she had since high school. Therefore, Bettye applied for fellowships during her senior year. Consistent with her ambitious approach, she applied at Yale, Harvard, the University of Iowa, and the University of California, Berkeley. She was rejected by the Ivy League schools but accepted by the two universities. The "coveted fellowship" at Berkeley had greater appeal because it was more prestigious and lucrative. She received $600 from Smith College, and another $1,125 from Berkeley. Once she decided on Berkeley, she danced the appropriate jig of joy: Once again, she had gained recognition for her intellectual acumen.

Bettye Goldstein graduated from Smith College on June 9, 1942. It was an event marked by mixed emotions. On graduation day, Bettye took great pride in her achievements as a student and as a journalist. She realized even greater pride when she overheard a college administrator tell her mother that her daughter had achieved the most outstanding record of any student who had ever matriculated to Smith. Among Bettye's many accomplishments, said the administrator, was that her honor's thesis represented "an original contribution to the field of behavioral science."

Bettye also felt a great void on graduation day: Her father decided not to come because of his poor health. Since the mid-1930s he had suffered from high blood pressure and a heart condition, and he could no longer walk without a cane. Upon learning of her father's decision, Bettye telephoned, begging him to come. He refused but offered a brighter side: She and her mother would not be embarrassed by his stubborn Jewish accent. Perhaps his comment was made in jest, perhaps out of bitterness. Either way, Bettye deeply felt her father's absence at an event that offered her public recognition for her accomplishments. In many ways, these accomplishments could be traced back to their conversations when they, as equals, explored ideas, issues, and current events.

Bettye also felt another loss. She would now leave Smith College, the small world where she had done so well and been so comfortable. Smith had become a safe haven. It had given her the emotional and intellectual space to rid herself of childhood insecurities, nourish her intellectual curiosity, and define herself in terms of her own values, rather than values imposed on her by others.

By the end of college, Bettye was well aware of her achievements. But she also knew she was something more. The four-year process of exploring the life of *her* mind had convinced her that she had the moral responsibility to use her education and talents to improve the lives of the next generation. From this realization, Bettye Goldstein knew she had to march in protest against any and all acts of injustice against those who suffered discrimination. And march she did.

3

Working for the Revolution

After the war, I had been very political, very involved, and consciously radical. Not about women, for heaven's sake! If you were a radical in 1949, you were concerned about the Negroes, and the working class, and World War III, and the Un-American Activities Committee and McCarthy and loyalty oaths, and Communist splits and schisms, Russia, China and the UN, but you certainly did not think about being a woman, politically.

Betty Friedan, "The Way We Were," 1974

In June 1942, Bettye Goldstein returned to Peoria, proud of her achievements at Smith College and excited about future challenges at the University of California, Berkeley. Her greatest joy came from knowing that she had left Peoria four years earlier as a precocious, insecure young woman but had returned as an educated, self-assured adult. To assert this new confidence, she declared independence from her past by dropping the final "e" from her first name. Next, *Betty* found ways to seek closure to her difficult childhood and adolescent years in Peoria. Two invitations made this possible.

The first invitation came from her mother. Miriam Goldstein, brimming over with pride about her daughter's achievements at

Smith College, arranged for Betty to give a lecture to a Jewish woman's group. Betty decided to challenge her listeners to think about their identity as Jews, a challenge she had faced and resolved at Smith College. In her remarks, she suggested that they make their Jewishness part of their identities, rather than give into the temptation to disguise it so they could "fit in." The second invitation came from Betty. She discovered that her former friends no longer considered her as an outsider; that the past "sorority-and-fraternity thing" no longer mattered. She wondered if college had made them all less prone to cliquish behavior or it might well be her increased confidence. No matter the reason, Betty celebrated her regained popularity by inviting her friends to a party at her house—and they all came.

Betty arrived in Northern California in late summer 1942. Most immediately the differences between Smith and Berkeley challenged her newly acquired self-confidence. Whereas Smith College was a small all-women's college in a New England town, Berkeley was a coeducational major research university in the San Francisco metropolitan area. Students at Smith numbered 2,000; students at Berkeley numbered 11,000 undergraduate and 2,000 graduate students. At Smith, Betty had been intellectually nurtured and challenged by James Gibson, Dorothy Wolff Douglas, and Eric Koffka. At Berkeley, she soon discovered that professors were more interested in pursuing their own scholarship than in guiding the intellectual development of graduate students. Finally, unlike Smith College, where a liberal arts education was a priority, Berkeley was embroiled with government-sponsored projects to develop technology and weapons for World War II. Most noteworthy was the work of physicist J. Robert Oppenheimer, whose research at Berkeley led to his appointment as scientific director of the Manhattan Project in 1942.

To make friends, Betty joined a study group of graduate students and faculty. Like her, members of this group were supporters of left-wing solutions to political problems; unlike her, many belonged to radical political organizations. In keeping with their radical ideas, group members decided to explore connections between Marxism and psychology, a challenging inquiry because

Marx rejected psychological theories as an explanation for historical determinism. More relevant to her adjustment to Berkeley, some members invited Betty to move in with them. Happily, she agreed. They lived in a large house near campus, which, to broadcast their political perspective, they named the "Red Castle." New friendships with like-minded graduate students helped Betty sustain her sense of confidence.

Clearly new friendships at Berkeley fanned the flames of Betty's emerging political passion, but the psychology department failed to ignite in her a desire to pursue an academic career. The exception was her studies with Erik Erikson, whose scholarship focused on using Freud's concepts to develop a theory of human stages of development from birth to death. At the time, Erikson's tutelage guided Betty to consider the implications of Freud's ideas on economic realities, which, she thought, might be the basis for her dissertation.

But overall, Betty was disappointed because graduate school lacked the rigorous coursework and faculty engagement she had encountered at Smith College. Her experience in a graduate symposium serves as the best example of this uninspired intellectual environment. At this gathering, Betty presented a summary of her honor's thesis for Smith College. Impressed by her work, one professor suggested that if she had not made her undergraduate thesis public, she could have used it as her graduate thesis.

At the end of her first semester, Betty was not sure she wanted to pursue a graduate degree in psychology. Perhaps, she should change directions, apply to medical school, and become a psychiatrist, an ambition she had had since high school. When she returned to Peoria at the semester break, Betty hoped to explore these questions with her father. But her hopes were dashed. In December 1942, Harry Goldstein was gravely ill.

Since the mid-1930s, Harry Goldstein had suffered from hypertension. Over the years, he had gradually reduced his hours at the jewelry store, spent winter months in Florida, and had become more intolerant about issues involving money. When Betty met with her father in December 1942, she discovered that he wanted to discuss his will, not her future. Goldstein told his daughter he feared that if her mother was his primary beneficiary, she would squander all his money. Therefore, he had decided to divide his inheritance among his wife and three children, and he wanted Betty to be the executrix of his estate. Without hesitation, Betty responded: It would be wrong not to make her mother the primary beneficiary and executrix, and she was not interested in his money. Once the issue of her father's will had been discussed, she asked his advice about applying to medical school. Goldstein's response was equally quick and definitive: He dismissed her idea, stating that her life would be wasted if she became "just another doctor."

Betty's conflicts with her father continued for the rest of semester break. As a consequence, she left Peoria in early January without saying goodbye, an action she soon regretted. On January 11, 1943, Harry Goldstein died. Betty went back to Peoria but refused to display grief at his funeral. Once she returned to Berkeley, however, she deeply mourned her father's death. She, his confidante and favorite child, had let her temper get in the way of spending quality time with her father when it was clear that he was dying.

In the second semester at Berkeley, Betty continued her graduate work and actively dated. That semester, she made a calculated decision to "lose her virginity." Her favorite suitor was Bob, the brother of one of her friends. (Friedan never revealed Bob's last name.) She especially liked the times when they went to San Francisco to sneer at "liberals" and to join the picket lines in a longshoremen's strike. That semester, Betty also kept wondering if a graduate degree in psychology would lead to a meaningful profession.

On March 27, 1943, Betty Goldstein no longer had the luxury of indecision: She received the Abraham Rosenberg Research Fellowship, the most lucrative grant awarded to a graduate student in the sciences. In addition, this fellowship had never been awarded to a woman or to a student in the psychology department. The awards committee gave her two weeks to accept or reject the fellowship. Betty rejected the fellowship, telling the committee that she had decided to give up her career in psychology to "work for the revolution." But was promoting radical change her primary reason?

In future writings and interviews, Betty Friedan claimed that she rejected the fellowship because accepting it meant she had to choose between a career in psychology and her relationship with Bob. When she told her lover about the graduate fellowship, Bob responded with an implied ultimatum: If she accepted the fellowship, she would damage their relationship. His reason was that he would never be given such a prestigious award, which suggests that he felt intellectually inferior. Faced with this ultimatum, Betty chose love over a career: She gave up the fellowship.

Such a scenario is plausible and certainly straightforward. However, the reality is that Betty's decision to give up the fellowship is more complicated than "love over a career." She was disenchanted with graduate school and tempted to apply to medical school so she could become a psychiatrist. In addition, she discovered that graduate school was far less compelling than issues facing industrial workers and minorities in wartime America. So when she told the awards committee that she decided not to accept the fellowship because she wanted "to work for the revolution," she acted on her political passion and her commitment to be honest with herself.

In the summer of 1943, Betty left Berkeley and moved to New York City. She had no job, but she had friends from Smith College who invited her to move in with them. They lived in an apartment in Greenwich Village, the gathering place for those who wanted to live the so-called bohemian life of radical politics and liberated sexuality. Once settled, Betty started looking for a job. Not knowing where to begin, she contacted a friend at the Highlander Folk School. From this query, she received several suggestions, including the Manhattan office of the *Federated Press* (*FP*). Within a few weeks, she was hired by *FP* for $30 per week as assistant news editor, a position she held until June 1945.

Working at *FP* met Betty's objective to "work for the revolution." Started in 1919 by members of the Socialist Party and militant trade unions, *FP* became the most successful left-wing news service in the 1930s and 1940s. Its editorial policies and articles, some of which Betty would write, advocated the rights of workers and the end of discrimination based on gender and race. From its political position, the news agency criticized policies of the Roosevelt administration because these actions muzzled workers' rights to strike during World War II. Thus, after her brief encounter with the ivory tower of graduate school, Betty once again found herself embroiled in political issues that she had supported in student publications at Smith College.

Once hired by *FP*, Betty had to straddle two contrasting worlds: On one hand, she was committed to advocating revolutionary changes for the working class. On the other, she enjoyed the privileges of her social class. She and her roommates were intellectuals and social snobs; they belonged to the upper middle class and had attended an elite private college. As young single women living in Greenwich Village in the 1940s, Betty and her friends convinced themselves that being liberal was too tame, too timid, and absent of revolutionary change. For them, attending meetings and rallies of communist-front organizations and singing revolutionary songs while sitting on the floor exemplified ways to rebel against the narrow bourgeois (middle-class) world of their parents. But when it came to scaling back on their lifestyle, these wannabe revolutionaries drew the line: As revolutionaries, they would need to reject capitalism, which meant they could no longer shop at the most expensive department stores for the latest fashions. That they could not do.

Though the contradiction might seem trivial, Betty had difficulty with the inconsistencies between her two diverse worlds. As a news editor for *FP*, she worked for the "revolution" that she, as an individual, did not fully support. During these early months in New York, Betty also still struggled with the loss of her father. The combination of these challenges led to frequent asthma attacks, writer's block, and periodic bouts with depression. Worried that she might have a nervous breakdown, Betty decided to see a psychiatrist. To pay for her therapy, she asked her mother for money from her father's inheritance, which her mother sent. Her visits to the psychiatrist relieved her immediate symptoms, but Betty learned that confronting her deeper psychological problems would be a long process.

Another tonic that soothed Betty's anxiety came from interactions with coworkers. At work, she made new friends—men and women who shared her passion for using journalism to broadcast radical ideas. When the workday ended, they often adjourned to the bar in the Newspaper Guild building. Over drinks, they explored the potential of a radical revolution for the rights of workers and minorities and made cynical comments about the "status quo." In these exchanges, Betty traded ideas with other left-leaning liberals like herself as well as with communists, socialists, and pacifists. Some interactions were more personal. Because she worked in the hurly-burly world of left-wing journalism, she knew people tuned into radical solutions for problems, such as terminating an unwanted pregnancy. When some of her friends from Smith, now pregnant, wanted an abortion, then illegal, Betty asked her colleagues at *FP* for contacts, which she passed on to her friends.

Working for *FP* allowed Betty to gain confidence as a journalist and to test her commitment to radical politics. Equally, it gave her a chance to take on the persona of a liberated woman, one who no longer subscribed to the social dictum of the double standard that women safeguard their sexual purity until marriage while men were free to engage in premarital sex. Betty had several short-term relationships with men, most of whom were married. Although these encounters never led to love and commitment, Betty discovered she was a passionate, sexually attractive woman—knowledge she needed to overcome her own insecurities. Her frequent liaisons also became more private: Most of her friends in the Greenwich Village apartment had married. Now without roommates, Betty relocated to a one-bedroom basement apartment that had a terrace but no kitchen.

Beyond drinks, arguments over tactics for the "revolution," contacts for abortions, and short-term affairs, Betty, at 23, earned the respect of her male coworkers at *FP*. Although she had limited exposure to the labor movement and the dynamics of power politics within specific unions, she learned quickly. Robert Schrank, a coworker and union organizer, remembers that it was Betty who taught him how to write and edit. Speaking in "rapid staccato" and assuming the role of a "tough but friendly Jewish mother," she impressed him with both her talent and seriousness. After he had written his first editorial, Schrank remembers that Betty told him always to write as though he was speaking to an audience: "Listen to your inner voice and write it down," she advised.

Betty Goldstein practiced what she preached. Her articles for the *FP* demonstrated that she empathized with the plight of workers even though she had never worked in a factory. Most especially, Betty devoted considerable attention to women's situations as workers, housewives, and consumers. She was assigned to write "Wartime Living," a regular column that targeted women workers or wives of union members. Part of the requirement was to offer a recipe in each column, a challenge because she was not an expert cook. At one point Betty got into trouble when she called for a tablespoon, instead of a teaspoon, of salt for a cake recipe. Betty's advice to women as consumers was far more successful because she made concepts like "price control" and "inflation" understandable and relevant to her readers. She attacked the federal government for giving into pressure from big business when, in one column, she told readers that the price of butter would increase because the government had given into the American Dairy Association's demand to end price controls and rationing.

Soon after she was hired by *FP*, Betty wrote one of her most significant articles which was based on an interview with Ruth Young. Young was an official at the United Electrical, Radio and Machine Workers of America (UE), a radical labor union that fought for economic equality for African American and women workers. In Young's view, women were being pressured to support World War II by working full time in wartime industries. Yet the government had made no provisions for the daily needs of their families, such as controlling escalating prices on food and housing and providing child care. Young states that many working women decided to quit because they lacked the energy to sustain the double shift as worker and homemaker. In response, the Roosevelt administration decided to "pin up" thousands of glamor posters designed to lure more women into factories. Under the headline "Pretty Posters Won't Stop Turnover of Women in Industry," Betty uses her interview with Young to argue that the federal government needed policies to address the difficulties working women faced, rather than spending money on glamour posters. She also allows Young to make the point of gender equality in the workplace: Young states that "women can do any job in the union, if they have the chance, anything from negotiating a contract to directing a political action program."

Despite the quality of her work, Betty lost her job in 1945 because *FP* needed to cut staff because it had lost subscribers. *FP*, along with other left-wing publications, was caught in the cross-fire of Cold War politics and anticommunism that defined the political culture of the United States at the end of World War II. The majority of Americans had long objected to the claim made by Karl Marx that workers should unite, take over the means of production, and redistribute the profits of industry equally because Marx's scenario threatened a free-market economy guided by the law of supply and demand. Most citizens became even more alarmed by the Soviet communism that began with the Bolshevik Revolution in 1917 and continued with the collectivization, five-year plans, and strong-armed tactics of Josef Stalin in the 1920s and 1930s. Although the United States and the Soviet Union set aside their ideological differences to join together in fighting fascism in World War II, this partnership, based on survival, ended when Germany surrendered in April 1945. Emerging from World War II were two superpowers—the United States and the Soviet Union. Each nation had the power, the natural resources, and the will to impose its political ideology on weaker nations.

To combat Soviet communism, the United States adopted a policy of containment, which meant it would use its economic and military resources to keep the Soviet Union from extending its reach into noncommunist countries. Within the context of containment, many Americans feared the infiltration of communism in the United States. This fear was based, in part, on the reality that the Communist Party of the United States of America (CPUSA) increased its membership through the 1930s, reaching a peak of 50,000 members by 1942. As a political force, the CPUSA had also influenced the political perspectives of left-leaning liberals, such as Betty Goldstein, as well as leaders and members of industrial trade unions.

By the 1950s, this intense anticommunist suspicion in the United States was labeled McCarthyism. The term emerged from the actions of Joseph McCarthy, a Republican senator from Wisconsin. McCarthy's involvement with the cultural phenomenon that would bear his name began with his speech to the Republican Women's Club of Wheeling, West Virginia. In this speech, he held up a piece of paper and told his audience that he held his hand a "list of 205 people that were known to the Secretary of State as being members of the Communist Party, and, who, nevertheless, are still working and shaping the policy of the State Department." Though the senator's claim had no basis, McCarthy's allegation led to a wider dragnet in which many individuals, mostly those employed by government agencies, the entertainment industry, and higher education, were accused of being communists or "fellow travelers" (communist sympathizers). These potential enemies were subjected to aggressive investigations and questioning before various government or privately run panels, committees, and agencies; the most active was the House Un-American Activities Committee (HUAC).

Irrespective of the politics of domestic anticommunism, Betty Goldstein, now out of work, needed a job. Relying on her track record at *FP*, she applied for a position at the *UE News,* the newsletter of the United Electric, Radio and Machine Workers of America. As she learned from her interview with Ruth Young, the union was at the forefront of the working-class revolution. Clearly biased toward radical actions by labor unions, the UE used its newsletter to advocate socialism and communism to promote economic, political, and social equality for working-class Americans. Moreover, *UE News* attacked American capitalists who were the stockholders and board members of Westinghouse and General Electric. Finally, using flagrant polemical rhetoric, reporters at the *UE News* pointed accusatory fingers at Joseph McCarthy, Richard Nixon, and Harry Truman, calling them politically ambitious villains who used "red baiting" to muzzle and quell dissent from labor union officials and workers.

To prove her commitment to radical change, Betty extolled her skills as a writer "who is able to describe with sincerity and passion the hopes, the struggle and the romance of the working people who make up most of America" in her job application. *UE News* hired Betty in the summer of 1946, a job she kept until late 1952. Once hired, she made an impression. Those who worked with her recall that she literally bubbled over with energy, often talking in spurts and rarely finishing a sentence because her mind raced so fast the words could not keep up. During her tenure at *UE News*, Betty covered a broad scope of issues. In 1947, she reported on the HUAC investigation of communist influence in Hollywood, which she damned. In 1948, she reported on the convention of the emergent left-leaning Progressive Party's nomination of Henry Wallace, which she celebrated.

As she had at *FP*, Betty primarily focused on low wages and job discrimination of women workers at *UE News*. When assigned to cover labor strikes, she reported the impact of strikes on the families as well as on the workers. In February 1947, she reported that the prices housewives paid are not based "on statistics or wishful thinking but day-to-day experience in the grocery store with a limited amount of money to spend and a constant number of mouths to feed." In March 1951, she returned to this theme, by pointing out that working women have the dual struggle: As workers they earned little, and as consumers they had to make sure their families had enough to live on. In September 1951, Betty told readers of the union's commitment to fight job discrimination against women in the column "It's a Union That Fights for all Workers." She begins by quoting a Latina: "Sometimes I think women need a union even more than men because the boss tries to take advantage of women more." That same year, Betty also covered a UE labor strike at a manufacturing plant in New Jersey, where most workers were women. Impressed by her coverage, union officials asked her to write a pamphlet that detailed job discrimination of women workers and the union's actions to end this inequality.

Published in June 1952, *UE Fights for Women Workers* represents Betty Goldstein's strongest argument for women workers as a labor journalist. She begins the 39-page pamphlet by peppering readers with labor statistics from the 1950 census that document wage discrimination. She writes that even though women are assigned jobs that involve "greater physical strain and skill" than most jobs done by men, they are "paid less than the underpaid sweeper, the least skilled man in the plant." By paying lower wages to women, Betty notes, U.S. corporations save a "staggering total of 5.4 billion dollars per year," which adds to company profits. Next, she ratchets up her argument against corporate America by quantifying that wage discrimination is even "more shocking" for "Negro women workers." Betty points out that 41.4 percent of married Negro women need to work because racial discrimination keeps their husbands "at the bottom of the pay scale." In addition, Negro women workers also experience racial discrimination because their job prospects are most often limited to "low-paying domestic work in private homes or menial outside jobs as janitresses and scrubwomen." As a consequence, Negro women earn an average of $474 a year. By comparison, white women workers earn an average of $1,062 and white male workers earn an average of $2,844.

After citing government statistics to prove job and wage discrimination, Betty zeroes in on her purpose: the commitment of United Electrical, Radio and Machine Workers (UE) to end such discrimination for women workers. Whereas Westinghouse, General Electric, and other corporations "keep women . . . in separate lower paying jobs," as a strategy to "drive down wages" in their workforce, the union is "determined to wage a fight that ends the double wage standard" by pressing for specific changes.

Betty concludes her pamphlet by enumerating the UE's Program for Women:

> Reslot all jobs by women up from common labor rates, under a single rate structure, to eliminate discrimination as compared to jobs done by men
>
> Post all job opportunities for upgrading according to seniority, regardless of race or sex, providing adequate training for women to qualify for new job openings.
>
> Make the company provide adequate health and safety safeguards for all workers.
>
> Eliminate double seniority lists for men and women wherever they exist.
>
> Give special attention to problems of married women growing out of family responsibility, such as shifts and absenteeism.

Eliminate discriminatory hiring practices against married women, Negro women, etc., where they exist.

Campaign for government-financed child care centers for working mothers as were provided in World War II.

Press fights against speedup which is causing accidents and ill health among women workers.

Guarantee the life and militancy of the union by developing, training and electing women to all levels of leadership.

See that Fair Practices Committees are functioning in every shop.

Clearly, the intent of these demands was to extend workers' rights to include women. By taking this position, the UE departed from the traditional position of labor unions such as the American Federation of Labor (AFL), which advocated policies that kept women in lower paying jobs. Thus, at the time, most readers of this pamphlet would have interpreted these demands as part of the radical agenda for the working class. And this was Betty Goldstein's intent.

In hindsight, this list also pours the foundation for the feminist perspective for women's full equality. When she authored the pamphlet in 1952, Betty did so as a self-conscious radical. As a consequence, this exposure to and articulation of the needs for women workers took root in her evolving political perspective. The UE's plan to end discrimination was a precursor to the affirmative action programs in the 1960s that Betty advocated. More significantly, the list of demands offered by UE to its women workers became an essential part of the agenda of the National Organization for Women (NOW), one written and promoted by Betty Friedan.

Homeward Bound

The revolution was obviously not going to happen ... in America by 1949: the working class wanted those pressure cookers, too.... In 1949, McCarthyism, and the reality of U.S. imperialism, corporate wealth and power all made men and women who used to have large visions of making the whole world over uncomfortable with the Old Left rhetoric of revolution.

Betty Friedan, "The Way We Were," 1974

In her high school autobiographical essay, "Through a Glass Darkly," Betty Goldstein declared she wanted to marry and have children. But she had conditions: She also intended to have an "absorbing interest" outside the home that brought her "success and fame." By the mid-1940s, her work as a labor journalist had met her desire for an absorbing interest, and within the small circle of radical union members, she had achieved success and fame. But now in her mid-twenties, she longed to find someone she loved and wanted to marry. When a coworker arranged a blind date for her with his close friend, Carl Friedan, Betty soon discovered that her high school wish had been granted: In 1947, she married Carl Friedan, and in their 22-year marriage they had three children.

"He brought me an apple and told me jokes" Betty later remarked, somewhat nostalgically, about her first date with Carl. She was also pleased he was handsome, intelligent, charming, sociable, and Jewish. On their first date—and those that followed in quick succession—Betty learned that Carl shared her passion for the theater, which he had also developed as a teenager. Growing up in the Boston area, Carl had spent his free time at vaudeville shows, learning to perform magic tricks. After high school, he studied play writing, acting, and directing at the Boston campus of Emerson College, a private college devoted entirely to the arts. He quit college and joined the army in World War II. As a soldier, Carl kept active in theater productions by working as technical director for the Mickey Rooney Soldiers Show Company. After the war, he moved to New York City to pursue a career in the theater. When he met Betty, Carl produced plays for summer stock in New Jersey and experimental productions in New York City.

Although mutual interests provided an entrée to their relationship, Betty and Carl soon realized they had much more in common. Both were exceptionally intelligent, wanted careers in nontraditional professions, and were interested in left-to-radical solutions to social and economic problems. Both struggled equally to overcome the impact of their mothers, and both believed that marriage could solve their overpowering emotional needs. They loved detective stories and the beach, and they were sexually attracted to one another. After a few dates, they became lovers, and within a few months, Carl moved into Betty's one-bedroom apartment.

Nine months after he charmed her with an apple and his jokes, Carl Friedan married Betty Goldstein, not once, but twice. Legally the couple was married on June 12, 1947, at New York's City Hall. A few months later, they had a traditional Jewish ceremony. This second ceremony was imposed by Carl's mother, Matilda Friedan. She insisted that her son have a Jewish wedding and demanded that this ceremony be in Boston, where she lived. Matilda also expected that the bride's family would pay for the ceremony. Miriam, Betty's mother, now remarried, complied. That the traditional ceremony was in Boston meant that many of Betty and Carl's friends, who lived in New York, could not come. Consequently, most guests were friends and relatives of the Friedan family. Betty's mother came, as did her sister Amy. Harry, Betty's brother, could not because he was in the army. To compensate for Harry's absence, Grandfather Horwitz, now in his 80s, came to Boston, proudly wearing his American Legion hat for the ceremony and reception. He was the hit of the wedding, much like a character in a Gilbert and Sullivan musical, noted Carl Friedan.

Later, Betty Friedan wrote that she did not enjoy this second wedding ceremony because her mother-in-law had dictated the terms of the event. What Betty did enjoy, however, was their honeymoon. In late summer 1947, the newlyweds borrowed a car equipped with a tent, two sleeping bags, a charcoal grill, and detailed maps of New England. They slept on the beach, hiked in the mountains, canoed on lakes, and, at night, heard bears.

Once summer ended, the Friedans nestled into married life. Betty continued working at *UE News* earning a regular salary (see Chapter 3). She also kept "Betty Goldstein" as her official byline. Carl divided his energies between organizing theater productions in summer stock and producing small-time off-Broadway productions in New York in the nonsummer months. Because both enterprises were entrepreneurial, his income was limited and inconsistent. The couple lived in Betty's one-bedroom basement apartment that Carl improved by building a bar out of a barrel to hide the sink in the makeshift kitchen. The Friedans enjoyed their bohemian lifestyle, often hosting parties for Carl's theater friends.

The Friedans decided to mask this lifestyle when they traveled to Peoria for the wedding of Betty's brother Harry in the fall of 1947. To fit in with the ambiance of the upscale lavish event, Betty decided to wear a stylish and expensive suit, an item she had to buy on credit because of her meager salary at *UE News*. Betty and Carl enjoyed themselves, especially at the wedding reception. While in Peoria, they visited some of Betty's high school friends, who were not only married but also parents. Now 27, Betty asked herself if she should now think about having children. She and Carl realized that they had no money and lacked secure professions. Disregarding practical considerations, they decided to begin a family. Within a few months, Betty was pregnant, and Daniel, the first of the Friedans' two sons, was born on October 3, 1948.

While pregnant, Betty continued to work full time at *UE News*. At the same time, she devoted attention to her future role as a mother. She took classes in natural childbirth, decided to breast-feed her baby, and arranged a year-long pregnancy leave with *UE News*, although she was only entitled to six weeks of full-time pay. As a future father, Carl attended classes with Betty on natural childbirth and remodeled their apartment to accommodate a child. When Daniel was born, Carl and Betty designed his birth announcement as a theatrical ad: "A Friedan Production" was its banner, and underneath, "Carl & Betty present Daniel Harry Friedan/World Premier Oct. 3rd, 1948." Betty enjoyed being a new mother. She wheeled her son in the park and learned about motherhood by reading Benjamin Spock's *The Common Sense Book of Baby and Child Care* (1946), the bible of parents in the baby-boom generation that followed World War II. No doubt, she felt more secure when she read, "Trust yourself. You know more than you think you do."

Yet the decision to have a child created conflicts between the Friedans. Because most of Betty's pregnancy leave was unpaid, Carl became overwhelmed by the financial responsibility to support his family. His desire to "make it" in theater evaporated; he no longer had the luxury of hoping that his summer stock productions would lead to productions on Broadway. Instead, Carl had to listen to his wife's endless carping that he should get a job in television or the public relations business. To meet these responsibilities, he gave up his dreams. Initially Carl settled for publishing an annual guide, *Summer Theater Handbook*, and, soon after, he started a small advertising agency.

Like Carl, Betty was also challenged by her new role as a parent. *UE News* asked her to return to work after 11 months. Immediately she needed to wean Danny and find a "motherly" person to care for him during the day. Betty was conflicted. She felt guilty about leaving Danny when she went to work. At the same time, she was committed to her job. So, like so many new mothers, Betty had to negotiate her work schedule. She spent early mornings with her son, arrived at work midmorning, skipped lunch to get errands and shopping done, and then left for home by 5 P.M. Thankfully, Betty was a fast and competent writer, so the abbreviated workday produced no complaints. However, she now resisted assignments that required travel and overnight stays.

At this point, the Friedans realized they needed to move because their one-bedroom basement apartment was too crowded. Initially, they rented an older roach-infested two-bedroom apartment on the edge of Harlem. Not satisfied, Betty kept searching for a better option. In the early fall of 1950, she read an article about Parkway Village, a 40-acre complex in the northeastern section of Queens that had been developed for employees of the United Nations (UN). What caught her attention was that Parkway not only had a cooperative nursery school, which would be perfect for Danny, but it also had set aside 200 units for ex-GIs and newspaper correspondents, which meant that they qualified. Within the next few days, the Friedans took the hour-long bus and subway ride from Manhattan to Parkway Village. They discovered that as a residential community, its 2,000 residents, mostly UN personnel, came from more than fifty countries and included diplomats, African Americans, and American Jews. Also the Friedans learned that Parkway Village, located in urban New York, had been designed as a typical suburban community: Stores were clustered in a town center, winding tree-lined streets traversed the residential neighborhoods, and homes ranged from two-storied brick houses with tall colonial columns to more modest four- to five-room garden apartments. Pleased by what they found, the Friedans leased a four-and-a-half-room garden apartment that became their home for the next six years.

Although concerned that the monthly rent of $118.50 stretched their tight budget, Betty and Carl were ecstatic about their new home. Coming from cramped, aging apartments in the city, they considered their garden apartment to be enormous. They also liked its modern design features of parquet floors, ceilings molded with white plaster, and French doors that opened out to a grassy common area shared by families in the complex. This new living environment prompted Betty to embrace the activities of a suburban housewife. She arranged and rearranged furniture, and she decided to decorate with the trend-setting modern designs of inexpensive Eames plywood chairs, a wooden red rocking chair, and a free-form three-cornered dining table. Betty expanded her homemaking skills by experimenting with new recipes, although clearly not her forté, and she asked her mother for the family's sterling silverware, which Miriam sent. Thinking back on these years, Friedan observed that she and Carl had shed their bohemian lifestyle because they were suddenly "very interested in houses and *things*: chairs, tables, silverware." No longer did they use *bourgeois* as a pejorative term because they now shared the same middle-class values as their parents.

In her new environment, Betty felt great happiness as a home-maker. Such contentment, however, extended beyond her experiments with interior decorating and cooking. Its groundswell came from a sense of community with other families who also lived in their apartment complex. This group had much in common. As parents of small children, they were like-minded in their approaches to child rearing. As left-leaning political liberals, they shared the same concerns about the rabid anticommunist tactics of McCarthyism and the actions of the House Un-American Committee (HUAC). Betty and other mothers organized play groups for their children and helped out each other with babysitting. At the supermarket—a new entity in the early 1950s—Danny, now a toddler, squealed with happiness when he saw his playmates from the neighborhood and from nursery school.

Initially, the Friedans, as well as their neighbors, bought barbecue grills, and soon thereafter, they organized weekend cookouts on the grassy common area. The wives made dips to serve with potato chips, the husbands made martinis and grilled hamburgers, and the children played games on the grassy lawn. The adults sat in canvas chairs, enjoying one another's company and thinking about how beautiful their children looked as they played together in the twilight. As friends, this group became one another's extended family. Together, they celebrated Thanksgiving, Christmas, and Passover Seders and pooled their money to rent summer vacation houses at Lake George, north of Albany, or at Fire Island, an hour from Manhattan. Indeed, Betty and Carl, as well as their friends, felt lucky, hoping their happiness would last forever.

Betty loved being a mother. To her, Danny was a sheer delight, an unexpected, undeserved, and marvelous bonus. One

Betty Friedan and Danny in 1949. © The Schlesinger Library, Radcliffe Institute, Harvard University.

of her greatest joys was when Danny smiled when he first recognized her as his mother. She also wanted to have another baby. She and Carl did not want Danny, now approaching three, to be an only child, and Betty, now in her early thirties, worried that if she delayed, childbearing might be more risky and difficult. By early spring 1952, Betty was pregnant, and on November 27, Jonathan, the Friedans' second son, was born. Physically Betty's pregnancy had been easy, but emotionally it was not. She experienced two unexpected consequences indirectly related to her pregnancy: one personal and the other professional.

Once pregnant, Betty noticed that Carl became less attentive. He often stayed in the city, claiming he had to work late, and he turned away from her sexually. Betty discovered that Carl had initiated an affair with a woman he had been involved with prior to their marriage. Though the affair ended within a few months, its pain remained because Carl's infidelity had deeper causes. Before the affair, Carl and Betty had become increasingly unhappy with each other. Both strong willed and hot tempered, they fought continually. Money was the flash point of most confrontations. Carl's lack of a steady well-paid job led to Betty's constant nagging and resentment, ironic considering how she had hated her mother's tirades against her father about money. Jonathan's birth and their friends at Parkway helped them repair the cracks in their marriage, at least in the short term.

The professional consequence of her pregnancy was that Betty lost her job in the summer of 1952, an action she did not expect because her articles were well received. The implied reason that she was laid off was because she, now pregnant, planned to take a one-year pregnancy leave as she had when Danny was born. Betty belonged to the Newspaper Guild, the union for journalists, and as a member, she was entitled to this leave. In an attempt to get her job back, Betty decided to file a grievance with the Newspaper Guild. But the union's representative would not support her grievance because, in his opinion, it was her fault for getting pregnant. Betty interpreted that remark and the lack of the union's support as an example of sex discrimination in the workplace. Later, Betty Friedan wrote that this instance served as her "first personal stirring" of feminism.

That Betty was laid off because she was pregnant might have been true, but there were more complicated reasons than sex discrimination. By the early 1950s, the *UE News* had to cut staff because it had lost 50 percent of its subscribers. Subscribers were members of the radical labor union, United Electrical, Radio and Machine Workers of America. In the 1930s and 1940s, the bulk of the union's membership belonged to or sympathized with the Communist Party of the United States of America (CPUSA). With the advent of domestic anticommunism in the 1950s, the union was forced to purge these communists and fellow travelers, which numbered about two-thirds of its membership. Fewer members meant fewer subscribers. Thus the editor of *UE News*, faced with having to cut his staff, decided not to keep a writer who planned to take a year's leave.

After her anger subsided, Betty began to see that, in reality, she had a limited impact as a labor journalist. Her stories were read by those who already supported radical change. Thus, no matter the power of her articles, Betty felt frustrated that her work would not lead to broad-based actions to improve the conditions for working women and men. Moreover, she understood that McCarthyism and all its trappings not only had derailed any revolutionary changes for the working class but also demanded total conformity to the American way of life. Given this, she concluded that, in this political climate, the person who sustained the security and values of the nuclear family was considered essential, whereas someone who promoted radical causes was considered subversive. Such a realization made Betty, now mother of two children, aware that she was more important and necessary as a mother and wife than as a writer for a radical publication.

In 1974, Betty Friedan, in an article published in *New York* magazine, told readers about this shift in her perspective. "The concrete, palatable actuality of the carpentry and the cooking you could do yourself," she writes, "and the surprising effectiveness of the changes you could make happen in school boards and zoning and community politics, were somehow more real and secure than the schizophrenic and even dangerous politics of the world revolution." Suburbia and children served as the "comfortable small world" that she, as other women like her, "could really do something about, politically." Mothers could help their children be successful by helping them with their homework, whereas they had no control over the potential use of the atomic bomb and the spread of communism.

Interestingly, Betty Friedan's observations in 1974 anticipate the analysis presented by Elaine Tyler May in *Homeward Bound: American Families in the Cold War Era* (1988). For the early years of the Cold War, "amid a world of uncertainties brought about by World War II and its aftermath," May argues that the "self-contained home ... promised security in an insecure world and offered a vision of abundance and fulfillment." Americans worried more about internal dissent brought about by racial strife, emancipation of women, class conflict and familial disruption than about the threat from the Soviet Union because internal homegrown conflicts threatened unified support for long-standing American values. Thus, if the values that shaped the American way of life were weakened or lost, then the subversive ideas of communism, like a contagion, could attack and take over the social and moral fabric of American society and politics. Validating Betty Friedan's experience, Elaine May observes that Americans alleviated their fears by turning to the family "as a bastion of safety in an insecure world" because its stability appeared to be "the best bulwark against the dangers of the cold war." And it was the woman—as mother and wife—who guarded the door.

Although homeward bound, Betty continued to seek opportunities as a writer and social reformer. Liberated from the daily grind of commuting to work, Betty refocused, redirecting her intellectual energy toward community projects. She became editor of the community newsletter, *Parkway Villager*, transforming it from a chatty source of social events and cooking recipes to a publication that led a campaign against proposed rent increases, illustrated the positive social impacts of racial and cultural diversity within the community, featured women who successfully combined their domestic lives with their career aspirations, and offered a muted, yet apparent, critique of the politics of McCarthyism. More significantly, as editor and writer for *Parkway Villager*, Betty decided to identify herself for the first time as *Betty Friedan*, leaving behind her maiden name of Goldstein and refusing to become known as "Mrs. Friedan."

Now entrenched in this domestic sphere of influence, Betty Friedan also decided to write for women's magazines. To make a transition from labor journalist to freelance writer, she took a course in fiction writing at Queens College, located near Parkway Village. A friend introduced her to Marie Rodell, a literary agent. Initially, Friedan asked Rodell if she could use her contacts with editors of women's magazines to market one of her freelance articles. When Rodell successfully sold this article to *Glamour* magazine, Friedan hired Rodell as her agent and decided to embark on a career as a freelance writer for women's magazines, a career she sustained for the next 40 years.

By 1956, Betty and Carl Friedan had outgrown Parkway Village both emotionally and physically. Their close friends—their extended family—had made life at Parkway a meaningful, fulfilling experience. But now, as most of them decided to relocate to suburban communities, the Friedans no longer had an emotional attachment to Parkway Village. Also, they needed a larger home because Betty was pregnant again. The Friedans narrowed their search to Rockland County, in the lower end of the Hudson Valley region, a one-hour commute to the city. They signed a one-year lease on a refurbished stone barn in Sneden's Landing, a small upscale community on the west side of the Hudson River. They moved in April; one month later, Emily, their third child, was born.

Their home at Sneden's Landing was, as Friedan told an interviewer in 1990, "the most romantic place" she had ever lived. Their living area, located on the second level of the stone barn, had a great long stone-walled living room and dining room with one wall of glass French doors that showcased a view of the Hudson River and countryside. An indoor balcony was at one end of the dining room, a space that Betty appropriated as a place to write. Carl, who enjoyed gardening, planted a vegetable garden, and both believed they lived in a spectacular place.

Moving to suburbia, however, presented new challenges. Initially, Betty had to reactivate her driver's license because public transit in Rockland County was not as frequent and reliable as it had been in New York City. Never a good driver, she recruited a friend as a tutor, so she could pass the driver's test, which she failed three times before passing. Thereafter, she drove only when necessary.

She had a greater challenge in trying to balance the family budget. Living in suburbia added expenses, but their annual earnings stayed constant. At this time, Carl earned a fairly predictable $13,000 annually from his public relations firm, whereas Betty's earnings as a freelance writer ranged from $4,000 to $7,000 per year. They had anticipated some increased costs when they moved. The monthly rent of $600 was more than double what they had paid at Parkway Village, and they, now residents of suburbia, needed two cars. They invested in a new car, a 1956 Ford Station Wagon, and bought a "rusty old second hand Packard."

The expense that the Friedans failed to anticipate was the cost of heating their home during the winter months. When they leased this refurbished barn, they were unaware it lacked insulation. Thus the cost to heat their second-floor living area in the winter months was $1,800. To pay the heating cost, they charged their groceries at the local store, and Betty, to save money, turned down the heat and wore a heavy sweater and gloves when she wrote articles.

These unanticipated expenses created tensions between Carl and Betty. Betty, who managed the family's finances, was constantly worried about money. She believed their finances were getting worse because their monthly expenses often exceeded their income by a "constant thousand ($1,000) at least." Pressured by the shortfall, Betty worked harder to get articles published in women's magazines, a pursuit that meant an added expense of hiring a part-time housekeeper to give her unencumbered time to produce freelance articles.

At the end of the first winter at Sneden's Landing, the Friedans decided to purchase a home, a decision, in part, motivated by the hope that they could improve their financial situation. Because they liked the small distinctive towns along the Hudson River, they searched for a house in these communities. Their search met with success: They purchased a spacious home in Grandview-On-Hudson, another small community of some 350 residents. Betty's inheritance from her father provided the down payment, and Carl's GI Bill provided a fixed low-interest loan.

Thus, like so many young families in the 1950s, the Friedans invested their future in the suburban lifestyle, even though their investment did not lessen their financial burden. Unlike many young families that purchased homes in tract housing, the Friedans chose to purchase a two-story Victorian mansion built in 1868 in Grandview, an upscale small community where most residents were members of the professional middle class. Thus, in essential ways, Betty Friedan's home was reminiscent of her childhood home in the Bluffs.

The Friedans' 1868 Victorian mansion had great potential but needed work. Overlooking the Hudson River, it stood on an acre of land of mostly ivy and woods. Their home had a spacious living room complete with French doors that opened out onto a front porch the length of the house, a large octagonal dining room, four fireplaces, and a graceful stairway that led to the four bedrooms. Excited by the potential of this Victorian mansion, Betty spent hours refurbishing it to its original state. She used paint remover to get down to the original marble on the fireplaces and the lovely wood on the stair banisters. On weekends, she, Carl, and the children went to various antique dealers and auctions to find furniture. One purchase, an oversized Victorian love seat, was one of Betty's treasured acquisitions.

Despite images of Betty Friedan spending hours to remove paint from fireplaces and comparison shopping for furniture, the future author of *The Feminine Mystique* was not a typical suburban housewife. Unlike her neighbors, Friedan integrated her role a homemaker with her ongoing commitment to pursue a career. Building on her initial success as a freelance writer for women's magazines, she had four articles published in 1956 and another two in 1957, thereby gaining credibility with editors of *McCall's, Good Housekeeping (GH),* and *Ladies' Home Journal (LHJ).* Consistently, Friedan submitted articles that departed from the "happy homemaker" stories that filled the pages of women's magazines. Instead she wrote articles that featured the experiences of ambitious independent women who achieved excellence in a career while raising a family. She also wrote articles that emphasized the importance of community-based child care as a means not only to enrich the social experiences of children but also to give mothers free time to pursue their individual interests. Like all writers, Friedan became frustrated with editors: More than once, they rewrote portions of her articles to better fit the magazines' formula of the "happy homemaker."

As a freelance writer, Friedan also made frequent trips into New York City. She met with editors and with her agent, Marie Rodell. She joined and attended monthly meetings of the Society of Magazine Writers (SMW), an organization for freelance writers that made her feel she was, indeed, "a real, honest-to goodness magazine writer." Her expertise also led to teaching writing courses at New York University (1958–59) and the New School for Social Research (1959).

Friedan's most successful article in the 1950s, ironically, had nothing to do with women. Friedan learned that scientists at Lamont Observatory, located near her home in Rockland County, had found evidence of a potential new ice age. She believed that details of their discovery might lead to an article for a mainstream general-interest magazine. After refreshing her high school grasp of geophysics and reading about recent scientific breakthroughs, Friedan interviewed the Lamont scientists.

She wrote her article, "The Coming Ice Age," as a scientific detective story. *Harper's*, a highly respected monthly magazine, published Friedan's article as its September 1958 cover story and included it in its anthology, *Gentlemen, Scholars and Scoundrels: A Treasury of the Best of Harper's from 1850* (1959).

Pleased by her success, Friedan enjoyed her work as a freelance writer: It required that she report, research, and write, activities she had relished since high school. Also, working as a freelance writer gave her, as a mother of three, the essential flexibility to meet the needs of her children, a reality that had equal value to her. Friedan organized play groups for her children and was assistant den mother for Danny's Cub Scout troop. Remembering how much she liked nature hikes as a Girl Scout, as assistant den mother, she often organized hikes along nature trails in the mountains of Rockland County, an activity far more interesting and meaningful than the "rote lessons" and games suggested by the National Council of the Boy Scouts of America.

Betty Friedan's commitment to meeting the needs of her children extended to monitoring the quality of their education. As an adolescent, Friedan had learned that education is fundamental to personal identity and public acceptance. From her experiences at Smith College, she had learned that a quality education opens up new intellectual perspectives and engenders independent thinking. Given these experiences, she became concerned when she learned that Danny, her eldest child, was bored in school. Danny had already shown that he, like his mother, was precociously bright, especially in mathematics. To make school more interesting, he solved arithmetic problems in unconventional and original ways. To his mother's dismay, Danny's approach led to being punished by his teacher. Protective of her son, Betty wanted to work with his teacher and the school administrators to make Danny's educational experiences positive and challenging.

At the same time that she learned about Danny's problems, Friedan was interviewing scientists at the Lamont Geological Observatory for "The Coming Ice Age." As she talked with the scientists, she wondered if it would be possible to organize a pool of scientists affiliated with the observatory, as well as other intellectuals living in Rockland County, for a series of weekend programs for students in the Rockland public schools. Always expansive in her ideas, Friedan envisioned that the resource pool could also include artists and writers, anthropologists and architects, and planners and professors who lived in Rockland County. Saturday programs might include conducting scientific experiments, painting murals, arguing law cases, and mentoring relationships between students and professionals. In the spring and summer of 1957, she began to write down her ideas about such a resource pool, which she labeled the "Intellectual Resources Pool," and gathered 15 women in her home to discuss ways to get the project off the ground.

Then in October 1957 her concept of an Intellectual Resources Pool gained a greater sense of urgency: On October 4 the Soviet Union successfully launched Sputnik I, the world's first artificial satellite. That the Soviets beat the United States in space led, in part, to a national debate over the crisis in education. In 1958, the U.S. Congress passed the National Education Defense Education Act, which funded stronger programs in higher education for the sciences and foreign languages and increased rigor in science and math in the K–12 public school curriculum.

Friedan immediately realized and acted on the connection between her concept of a resource pool and the national debate on education. She secured funds from the Rockland Foundation to launch the Intellectual Resources Pool and organized its first symposium, "America's New Frontier Is Intellectual." In part, attendees of the symposium learned that Friedan's program promised it would "help a younger generation meet the challenge of our new intellectual frontiers."

Once officially launched and funded, participants in the Intellectual Resources Pool readily acknowledged Friedan's leadership by appointing her project director, a position she held until 1964. In 1960, the New World Foundation, a group committed to supporting progressive causes, awarded the resources pool an annual grant that included a yearly stipend of $3,000 for Friedan as project director. The New World Foundation also required that the organization be renamed Community Resources Pool.

Under Friedan's leadership, the Community Resources Pool organized programs and symposiums for both students and adults. These meetings often made the case that the underlying problem with American public school education was the consequence of the demand for conformity by the Cold War politics of McCarthyism. Such a demand led to stamping out the free exchange of ideas—the very bedrock of progressive education. By shaping events with this left-to-the center political perspective, Friedan not only responded to the political perspective of the New World Foundation but also drew upon her exposure to radical ideas at Smith College and her work as a labor journalist.

Clearly establishing a resource pool of intellectuals that provided enrichment activities for students in the public schools was significant for Friedan and for residents of Rockland County. But its significance was much greater. What Betty Friedan created, organized, and nurtured became a model for similar efforts across the nation. With Sputnik as a catalyst, educators in the late 1950s and early 1960s focused on reinvigorating American education. Out of this came an organized effort to infuse innovative pedagogies, such as interdisciplinary learning, experimentation, learning by doing, and alternative educational systems, into the public school curriculum. Those who set such ambitious objectives must have welcomed the experiences and successes of the Community Resources Pool of Rockland County, a project that began when Friedan learned that her son was bored in school.

By the late 1950s, Betty Friedan had achieved the goals she had set as a high school senior: She was married to a man she loved, she had three healthy and happy children, she had a comfortable, upper-middle-class lifestyle, and she had a burgeoning career as a writer for women's magazines. Her pathway to achieve these goals had been defined by her exposure to and belief in political ideas based on extending social justice and increasing opportunities to those who lacked an equal voice in American society and politics because of their gender, race, ethnicity, and/or social class. Clearly, in her interactions with her family and friends, in her profession as a labor journalist and freelance writer for women's magazines, and in her leadership in the Community Resources Pool, Friedan had made her mark. But, in the late 1950s, she asked herself, "Is this all?" To answer this question, she had to confront the feminine mystique.

Defrocking the Myth

The insights, interpretations both of theory and fact, and the implicit values of this book are inevitably my own ... My answers may disturb the experts and women alike, for they imply social change. But there would be no sense in my writing this book at all if I did not believe that women can affect society, as well as be affected by it; that, in the end, a woman, as a man, has the power to choose, and to make her own heaven or hell.

Betty Friedan, *The Feminine Mystique*, 1963

Four months before the Soviet Union launched Sputnik I, making clear that it had superior technology to the United States in the "race for space," Betty Friedan had made clear to the Smith College alumnae attending the 1957 reunion that their college education had greater value than cooking, cleaning, and taking turns in carpools. Friedan pointed to evidence from their responses to a questionnaire that they had completed prior to the reunion. No doubt these women felt comforted and validated by Friedan's comments. But neither they nor she then realized that the "Smith College Anonymous Questionnaire for the Fifteen-Year Reunion" would be the impetus for defrocking the myth of the feminine mystique. Six years later, *The Feminine Mystique* was published as an indictment of America's system of sex inequality.

In early 1957, Betty Friedan volunteered to organize a survey for the 15-year reunion of her graduating class from Smith College (1942). As she considered possible questions, Friedan thought about her own life since college. Although she could list several achievements as a suburban housewife and freelance writer, she also felt she had not lived up to her classmates' expectations that she would do great things. Despite the fact she had graduated at the top of her class and had been awarded a prestigious graduate fellowship, she had quit graduate school, been fired from her job as a labor journalist, and now spent her time writing "happy homemaker" articles for women's magazines. Her personal life was not much better: She did not feel complete fulfillment as the wife of Carl and the mother of Danny, Jonathan, and Emily. Friedan's introspection made her wonder if her classmates felt the same.

Friedan was equally concerned by the broad-based acceptance of the theories of women's emotional well-being that had been presented by Freudian psychoanalysts Maryina Farnham and Ferdinand Lundberg in *Modern Woman: The Lost Sex* (1947). The essential cause of the modern woman's anxiety and unhappiness, they argued, was her attempt to break away from her natural role as wife and mother. The culprit in this road to neurosis was higher education because it shifted a woman's focus to an unnatural inclination for a career. The two experts stated that the "modern woman," an "unfortunate sex," was in "grave peril" because her intellectual interests would lead to a "masculinization of women." Such a shift had "enormously dangerous consequences to the home" that the children depended on, and "the ability of a woman, as well as her husband, to obtain sexual gratification." The ideas expressed in *Modern Woman* were widely debated well into the 1950s and led to a spate of articles published in mainstream magazines. As an example, *Life* magazine devoted a special issue on the "The American Woman: Her Achievements and Troubles" in December 1956. One article in this issue was "Changing Roles in Modern Marriage: Psychiatrists Find in Them a Clue to Alarming Divorce Rise." This article featured five psychiatrists from various locations in the United States, who agreed, based on their experience, that the consistent factor leading to divorce was when wives were not "feminine enough."

The ideas presented in *Modern Woman: The Lost Sex* also infiltrated into the political culture. Adlai Stevenson, the Democratic Party's candidate for president in 1952 and 1956, weighed in with his interpretation in his Commencement Address at the graduation ceremony at Smith College in 1955. Stevenson made clear that he disagreed with the conclusions in *Modern Woman*. Instead, he argued that college-educated women were better prepared to "inspire . . . a vision of meaning of life and freedom" by helping their husbands "find values that will give purpose" to their work and by teaching their children "the uniqueness of each individual human being." Such inspiration was essential, he implied, at a time when America was threatened, internationally and domestically, by the actions and communist ideology of the Soviet Union. In their future, Stevenson told graduates, as they "sat in the living room with a baby" on their laps or in the "kitchen with a can opener" in their hands, they should remember how their "humble role of housewife" will contribute much in the "crisis" of these troubled times.

Irrespective of the fact that Adlai Stevenson, unknowingly, couched his remarks within the comfort zone of the 1950s rendition of separate spheres, he indirectly dismissed a key conclusion of *Modern Woman*: That a college education damaged a woman's ability to be a good wife and a mother, to be psychologically and socially healthy, and to be sexually satisfied. It was Stevenson's emphasis—one that validated the value of higher education for women—that captured Friedan's attention. She questioned whether Stevenson was being fair. Friedan agreed that a college education made women better wives and mothers, but she disagreed with Stevenson that college-educated women should limit their contributions to American society to burping babies and cooking dinner.

Friedan wanted to find out whether her perceptions were shared by others in her graduating class. She recruited two former classmates, Marian (Mario) Ingersoll Howell and Ann Mather

Montero, to help with the survey; the trio met several times to discuss the focus and craft the questions. To prompt their classmates to think about how they saw themselves, the three women included standard questions to measure the socioeconomic factors and open-ended questions that prompted respondents to reveal whether they, as wives and mothers, were "truly satisfied" sexually, intellectually, and emotionally. The questionnaire was mailed to all graduates, and they were directed to give "an honest, soul-searching picture" of what they had become, to be "candid," and to "elaborate where the spirit" moved them. Two hundred women, less than half the class of 1942, responded.

As she tallied the results and analyzed the responses, Friedan realized that she had been right: Belying the theory promoted by *Modern Woman*, most respondents indicated that their education had not kept them from sexual fulfillment and the joys of motherhood. At the same time, however, their comments did not support Stevenson's claim that college-educated women were content with their role as the "humble housewife." Most respondents (74 percent) affirmed that their education had given them the vision and skills to organize and/or participate in community projects, to pursue their individual interests and talents, or to make plans for continued study and a career once their children had grown. The survey results also implied, in Friedan's view, that current theories about a woman's appropriate social role, ones that popularized Freud's theories, were inaccurate and damaged the emotional well-being of women. Friedan presented her report to her classmates at the 15-year reunion in June 1957.

After the reunion, Friedan decided that the Smith College survey responses would be appropriate as an article in a mainstream woman's magazine, so she sent a proposal to editors. The editors at *McCall's* magazine liked the idea and asked her to submit an article. To capture attention, she titled her article "Are Women Wasting Their Time in College?" Relying exclusively on her analysis of the Smith College survey, she answers "no." A college education is neither the cause of emotional problems, as suggested by *Modern Woman*, nor is its only purpose to prepare women to be better homemakers, as implied by the political culture. Instead, Friedan asserts, a college education gives women the ability to integrate their individual interests, avocations, and/or aspirations with their domestic role as wives and mothers. Said simply, Betty Friedan argued that women were entitled to a husband, children and, as she had believed since high school: to have the freedom "to do something unique with their lives—to have an absorbing interest."

The editors of *McCall's* believed they had agreed to an article that illustrated how college-educated women, as Stevenson had suggested, understood that their role as wives and mothers was essential during the Cold War. Instead, editors were presented with an article that asserted college-educated women were not only entitled to, but also should act on their right to expand their life beyond the home. Not liking what they read, the editors rejected Friedan's article. Shocked and angry, she sent the article to the *Ladies' Home Journal,* where its editors rewrote her article so its message was the opposite of her argument. Angered again, Friedan pulled the article and sent it to *Redbook.* After reading the article, Jim Stern, the magazine's editor, rejected the article, believing that Friedan, whose work he respected, had gone "off her rocker" because only the "most neurotic housewife" would identify with her article.

The day she received Stern's rejection letter, Friedan had to take her children to the pediatrician in New York City. On the subway, she read the letter and knew Stern was wrong. In fact, she told herself, all the magazine editors were wrong. At that point, she realized that no woman's magazine would publish her article because its message did not match the marketing strategy of women's magazines: to give women information that was useful, interesting, and nonthreatening. When she and her children got off the subway, Friedan called Marie Rodell, her agent, from a pay phone. She told Rodell to stop sending her article to women's magazines. She had decided to write a book and needed an appointment with George Brockway, an editor at W. W. Norton and Company. After she hung up, Friedan took her children to the doctor.

When she met with Brockway, Friedan described her research and explained why it warranted a book. Already impressed by her freelance articles and intrigued by her proposal, Brockway offered Friedan a book contract, agreed to a $3,000 advance, and expected the book in a year.

Now with a book contract, Friedan needed to find time to research, interview, and write while simultaneously meeting her family obligations and commitments as project director of the Community Resources Pool. Betty knew that she could not work at home because domestic tasks would be too disruptive. Now that Emily, her youngest child, was in nursery school, she could go to New York City three to four days a week. In the city, she found free workspace in the Frederick Lewis Allen Room at the New York Public Library. This workspace served as a retreat—no phones, no interruptions, and no domestic responsibilities.

Working at the New York Public Library also had added benefits: She could ask personnel to retrieve materials from the library's holdings, and she had a sense of belonging because other writers also worked in the Allen Room. Betty enjoyed the camaraderie with these writers, who were men, and often joined them for lunch. But they usually kidded her about writing a book about women, which implied her work was less worthy than theirs. Hurt by their dismissive attitudes, Friedan eventually pretended that she was too busy to have lunch with them.

After settling practical details, Betty Friedan started to expand her ideas for her book. To start, she needed to broaden her research beyond the 200 responses from the Smith class of 1942. Thus she decided to interview women at different stages of the life cycle—high school students, college students, young housewives and mothers, and women approaching middle age. She was clear about what she wanted to investigate: the attitudes and life styles of middle- and upper-middle-class women who lived in suburban communities. Over the next two years, Friedan had in-depth interviews with 80 women who, for the most part, lived in communities in the greater New York area and in the suburbs of Chicago and Boston. She regretted that lack of funds kept her from traveling to the southern and western states.

In these interviews Friedan learned that women's attitudes, at times, confirmed the results the Smith survey; at other times, their attitudes were different. When she interviewed seniors at Smith College in 1959, for example, Friedan learned that unlike those in the class of 1942, these young women were more concerned about an engagement that led to marriage than an engagement with intellectual growth, a change that dismayed her. When she interviewed young homemakers, Friedan discovered that they, unlike her Smith classmates, were not involved in meaningful activities outside the home. Instead, they often described themselves as feeling empty, incomplete, tired, or bored. That so many women expressed feelings of unhappiness and frustration bothered Friedan because she could not find the right words to define or label these feelings.

Then on an April morning in 1959, Friedan figured out how to articulate these amorphous feelings. That day she met with four women who lived in a suburban development near her home. While having coffee, one of the mothers, "in a tone of quiet desperation," said "the problem." Her simple statement resonated with her friends, who knew she was not talking about a problem with her husband, or her children, or her home. "Suddenly they realized," Friedan writes in *The Feminine Mystique*, "they all shared the same problem, the problem that has no name." Interviews with other young mothers confirmed that "the problem" was pervasive. As an example, Friedan talked with a woman who had quit college at age 19 to get married and have children. This young mother said, "I've tried everything women are supposed to do—hobbies, gardening, pickling, canning, and being very social with my neighbors.... I can do it all, and I like it, but it doesn't leave you anything to think about....But I'm desperate. I begin to feel that I have no personality. I'm a server of food and putter-on of pants and a bed maker, somebody who can be called on when you want something. But who am I?"

In addition to interviews, Betty Friedan turned her attention to women's magazines. As a freelance writer, she had become painfully aware that editors shaped content to perpetuate the myth of the happy homemaker. But she was unclear whether the editors' current attitudes had always been the case. To find out, Friedan did a comparative analysis of heroines of short stories that had been published in the *Ladies' Home Journal, McCall's, Good Housekeeping*, and *Woman's Home Companion* in the same months of 1939, 1949, and 1959. The result was startling.

The persona of heroines in the 1930s was of an adventurous, attractive, self-reliant woman marching toward a vision or personal goal. By 1949, the persona was a woman who gave up her career for the fulfilling life of a housewife. By 1959, the persona of women had no commitments outside the home or no interest in current events. Now heroines were younger, more childlike and dependent; they aspired only to marry and have children.

Such findings prompted Friedan to talk with editors about their changed policies. They told her that their readers would be interested in reading articles about politics, art, science, ideas, adventure, and education *only if* (emphasis added) these issues were presented in terms of their emotions as wives and mothers. For example, an editor revealed that he had considered printing an article, "How to Have a Baby in an Atomic Bomb Shelter" when developers decided to add bomb shelters in suburban homes. But when Friedan asked, this same editor admitted he had never considered publishing an article about the fact that the atomic bomb had the power to destroy the human race. Friedan also learned that editors of women's magazines were reluctant to print articles about how the civil rights movement in the southern states might impact the presidential election of 1960 because, noted these editors, the issue of racial discrimination had no relevance to their readers.

Interviews with editors prompted Friedan to compare content of nonfiction articles in women's magazines from earlier decades with content in the 1950s. Friedan found in the 1930s and 1940s that these magazines published a wide range of articles on political and social issues. Walter Lippmann wrote about American diplomatic relations; Harold Stassen and Vincent Sheean wrote about Stalin, the persecution of Jews in Germany, and the New Deal; Carl Sandburg, biographer of Abraham Lincoln, detailed the assassination of the Civil War president; and another writer told of Margaret Sanger's battle for birth control, an article that would never make it into a woman's magazine in the late 1950s, one editor told Friedan.

From her interviews and review of women's magazines, Friedan concluded that editors and advertisers were responding, in part, to the cultural impact of the Cold War. That they, as

Elaine Tyler May argues, were responding to a belief that the "sphere of influence" of the home served as the "domestic version of containment." Within the walls of the suburban home the bonds of the nuclear family could ward off the "potentially dangerous social forces" that threatened American society, which made women, as wives and mothers, essential to the success of domestic containment.

Although she learned from her investigative work that "domestic containment" had influence, Friedan did not accept it as the only, or even the most powerful, explanation for the social pressures on women to stay in their domestic sphere. Instead, she called on her academic training in psychology and her expertise as a journalist. What Friedan had learned from her training with "psychological giants" like Eric Koffka and Erik Erikson and from her work as a "hands-on-reporter" made her wonder, "What gives the feminine mystique its power?"

To answer this question, Betty Friedan examined the pervasive impact of Sigmund Freud's theories about human sexuality on American cultural attitudes. Specifically, Freud's twin theories that anatomy is destiny and the phenomenon of "penis envy" make women feel inferior to men. Freud argued that one's sex predetermines one's natural personality from infant to adult and that a girl child's discovery of the anatomical difference between herself and her brother cause her to feel that she and all women (including her mother) are lesser beings, incomplete males. The wish for a penis and the power it represents was central to Freud's view of women and girls. It explained why the "normal" female wants a husband and (male) child to compensate, and it accounted for everything in her personality: her neuroses, her self-absorption, her lack of originality and her underdeveloped ability to think rationally.

According to Friedan's interpretation, Freud and his followers missed the point. Most assuredly, girls and women felt inadequate, but a missing penis was not the cause. Rather, girls and women considered themselves deficient because they missed the privileges and opportunities for self-fulfillment outside the home that society gave their brothers and husbands. Said simply, the problem was not anatomy; it was how culture interpreted anatomy by constructing specific roles for men and women.

After reconsidering Freud, Friedan expanded her analysis by investigating the ways that his theories had shaped the assumptions in sociology and cultural anthropology. Sociologist Talcott Parsons, Friedan learned, had applied Freud's concepts to his theory of family stability. Parsons believed that clearly defined, sex-differentiated roles are essential to family stability, which implied that women who want to pursue careers and interests outside the domestic sphere would ruin that stability. Cultural anthropologist Margaret Mead also weighed in on the biology and identity issues. Friedan found that Mead, especially in her work of the 1940s and 1950s, glorified women specifically because of their biological function, demonstrating that she had interpreted anthropological data through the lens of Freudian theory.

With each new discovery, Friedan had a new set of questions. Consequently her quest to research her topic thoroughly is impressive. She considered the ideas expressed by Simone de Beauvoir in *The Second Sex* (1949) and the work of Freudian revisionists such as Erik Erikson and Abraham Maslow. She learned more about the first wave of the women's rights movement (1848–1920) and surveyed the content of the marriage and family textbooks targeted for high school and college students. Finally, Friedan examined women's images in magazine ads and television commercials, and she evaluated female characters in novels, television shows, and movies. Now, with her research completed, Friedan was ready to write her book.

Betty Friedan's central argument in *The Feminine Mystique* is that the modern woman's unhappiness, her "problem that has no name," is that she had been assigned to a "place" solely on the basis of her sex, and in that role, her essential (and only) function was wife and mother. Such limitations caused a woman to feel deprived because she could not develop an identity of her own, and she could not envision herself as a unique human being. Moreover, Friedan argues that a woman's willingness to accept her domestic role had been infused into her psyche by commentators and experts of American culture: She had been brainwashed into embracing the ideology of the feminine mystique.

By asking the question, "Is this all?" Friedan skillfully and powerfully defrocks the "modern woman" from her cultural wrappings of the feminine mystique. Friedan argues her case through the voices of those women she had interviewed, through a blistering commentary on the content and intent of women's magazines, and through attacks on the popularization of Freud's theories on human sexuality. Friedan asserts that advertisers manipulate women into believing they can achieve fulfillment by using the latest model vacuum cleaner or bleaching their clothes a purer white. She shows that women's magazines romanticize domesticity and present an image of women as "gaily content in a world of bedroom, kitchen, sex, babies and home." And she details how psychiatrists popularize the notion that any woman unhappy with a full-time occupation as housewife must be neurotic. Most damaging, Friedan argues that women's horizons are circumscribed at childhood by the assumption that their highest calling in life is to be a servant to her husband and children. In effect, the home has become a "comfortable concentration camp that infantilized its female inhabitants," forced them to "give up their adult frame of reference," and destroyed their minds and emotions.

After bombarding readers with examples, Betty Friedan offers a solution to "the problem that has no name" by answering "No" to the question, "Is this all?" Friedan's solution is the fortified self— the new woman. Borrowing heavily from Abraham Maslow's theory of self-actualization, she defines this new woman as a person who is secure, confident, self-aware, and committed to using her talents, capacities, and potentialities for her own self-fulfillment and in her interactions with others.

Because most women had not yet achieved self-actualization, Friedan, in her final chapter, outlines the process. With a sense of urgency, she writes, "the problem that has no name, the reality that American women are kept from growing to their full human potential, is taking a far greater toll on the physical and mental health of our country than any known disease." To end this potential epidemic requires "A New Life Plan for Women." Fundamental to this plan is the availability of a college education. It is this educational exposure, according to Friedan, that will enable a woman "to find herself, to know herself as a person by creative work of her own." Friedan writes, "What we need now is a national educational program, similar to the GI Bill, for women who seriously want to continue or resume their education—and who are willing to commit themselves to its use in a profession." Like the GI Bill for returning veterans, this program would provide "properly qualified" women with tuition and additional subsidies to defray other expenses such as books, travel, and, if necessary, some household help.

Betty Friedan finished *The Feminine Mystique* in the summer of 1962 and W. W. Norton published 3,000 hardcover copies in February 1963. Friedan celebrated her success by bleaching her hair blond and painting her living room a "euphoric purple." Though excerpts of the first two chapters had been published in women's magazines, *The Feminine Mystique* initially experienced limited sales, reviews, and promotional ads. George Brockway, who expected the book to lose money, resisted publishing additional hardcover copies, and he limited advertising to a handful of small ads in *The New Yorker*. The reviews were mixed. Many reviewers were enthusiastic, with only an occasional gripe about the drilling insistence of the style. Others criticized Friedan because she had made sweeping generalities, found data to support her preconceived conclusions, and ignored the reality that ancient customs, rather than Freudian theory, had created the attitudes and images of oppressed women.

Enormously proud of his wife, Carl Friedan, who had a successful public relations business, told Betty that the book needed to be promoted. After many calls and letters from Betty, a list of ideas from Carl, and increased sales of the book, Brockway agreed to print more copies of the book and hired an outside consultant to promote Friedan's book. This consultant arranged book tours and interviews on several television talk shows for Friedan. Although this exposure led to increased interest and sales, the biggest boost came when Dell Publishing Company purchased paperback rights for *The Feminine Mystique* in early 1964. At the end of that year, 1.3 million copies of the paperback edition had sold, making it the best-selling nonfiction paperback of the year. By 1970, 1.5 million copies of the paperback version of the book were in print, and Friedan had earned about $100,000 on the hard- and soft-cover sales.

Annoucement of appearance by Betty Friedan. © The Schlesinger Library, Radcliffe Institute, Harvard University.

Gerda Lerner, considered today as the pioneer of and leading scholar in women's history, was the first feminist to see both the value and limitations of Friedan's work. In February 1963, Lerner, who had recently initiated a new course, "The Role of Women in American Culture," at the New School for Social Research, wrote to Friedan. With sincerity, Lerner begins by telling Friedan that her "splendid book" has "done a most important job which desperately needed doing." It would most assuredly "unsettle a great many smug certainties" and "cause a lot of healthy doubts." She agrees with Friedan that the "experts" of the feminine mystique had had it "their way far too long," and hopes that Friedan's book would stir up considerable controversy because then people would begin to think of new solutions.

Then Lerner tactfully, yet clearly, shifts her focus to a critique of *The Feminine Mystique.* "You address yourself solely to the problems of middle class, college-educated women," Lerner notes. Though valuable for this specific group, such a narrow perspective had been one of the "shortcomings of the suffrage movement for many years" and had, in Lerner's view, "retarded the general advance of women." More specifically, Lerner reminds Friedan that "working women, especially Negro women, labor not only under the disadvantages imposed by the feminine mystique, but under the more pressing disadvantages of economic discrimination." Given that, leaving these groups of women "out of consideration of the problem" and ignoring "the contributions they can make toward its solution" is something that women activists "simply cannot afford to do." Working-class women, by their "desperate need, by their numbers, by their organizational experience" in trade unions are essential in "reaching institutional solutions to the problems of women." Honing in to make her point, Lerner tells Friedan that problems that face individual women cannot be solved "on the basis of the individual family." Rather solutions will only be found from the combined efforts of the larger "community" that includes working-class women and women of color.

In this critique, Lerner is the first to stir up controversy on Friedan's "splendid book." But her critique also paves the way to offer a "new solution" to the problems facing women. "I have in mind," writes Lerner, "not only the fine education scheme you suggested, but a system of social reforms [such as] daycare centers, maternity benefits, communized household services" that would be legislated and funded by the government. Lerner closes her letter by suggesting that someday they might meet to explore further the issues facing women and her own ideas for social reforms. Friedan and Lerner never met. But as president of the National Organization for Women, Friedan incorporated many of Lerner's "system of social reforms" into the organization's agenda and consistently argued for such reforms through the 1990s.

Gerda Lerner was right in her criticism. For the most part, Betty Friedan ignores women who, because of skin color, sexual preference, educational attainment, or socioeconomic circumstances, fall outside her experiences as a woman in American society. Another shortcoming is that Friedan implies that the ideas of "the feminine mystique" were a post–World War II phenomenon, when in fact they are an updated version of the nineteenth-century concept of separate spheres. She also leaves the impression that women in the 1950s were more victimized than they had been in the past, which is inaccurate, and she ignores women who were content with their lifestyles, 60 percent according to a 1962 Gallup poll. Moreover historian, Joanne Meyerowitz punches holes in Friedan's evidence. In "Beyond *The Feminine Mystique*: A Reassessment of Postwar Mass Culture, 1946–1958" (1993), Meyerowitz proves, through an analysis of nonfiction articles in women's magazines, that Friedan made exaggerated claims regarding the confinement of women in suburbia.

So why is *The Feminine Mystique* cited as a powerful tract that helped shape second-wave feminism? Journalist Mary Walton notes, "Friedan beamed straight into those boxy little houses in the Levittowns of America [when]she wrote, 'A baked potato is not as big as the world, and vacuuming the living room floor—with or without makeup—is not work that takes enough thought or energy to challenge any woman's full capacity. Women are human beings, not stuffed dolls, not animals.'" Implied by Walton, the power of *The Feminine Mystique* lies in how Friedan verbalized the unarticulated grievances of women living in suburbia. She did this by using a narrative style and by making recommendations that did not threaten homemakers. First, in her narrative, Friedan uses a coffee klatch vernacular to transmit her message. She unfolds her examples and evidence in a friendly, empathic, take-me-into-your-confidence tone used by women when they take breaks from their daily routines to have coffee with friends or when they read articles in women's magazines. With eloquence and passion, Friedan dramatizes through case studies the boredom and alienation of those afflicted by "the problem that has no name." By so doing, she not only crystallized the sense of grievances of women but also provided an ideological explanation, the "feminine mystique," with which they could identify. In addition, Friedan's solution—a GI Bill in education for women—is well within the comfort zone of middle-class values. And finally, though targeted for the middle-class homemaker, *The Feminine Mystique* resonated with women outside that sphere. Although working-class women and women of color were outsiders, many aspired to become part of middle-class America. In that way, Friedan's book became a primer of what women were supposed to feel and think.

Certainly Betty Friedan felt gratified that *The Feminine Mystique* was widely read and embraced by women. But writing the book became a deeper, more personal experience. She later told an interviewer that writing *The Feminine Mystique* was a "gut-writing ... transcending experience." Specifically, her process of gathering information, thinking through theories, and writing the book demanded that she confront long-standing and deeply felt conflicts with her mother. Before working on the book, Friedan had considered her mother as "castrated and useless—a woman always busy with a new committee, a new cause." Since childhood, she had been painfully aware of her mother's misery. But writing *The Feminine Mystique* caused Friedan to see that her mother, robbed of her own aspirations for college and career, had lived out her fantasies through her children, most especially her two daughters, Betty and Amy.

In spring 1963, Friedan decided to send her mother a first-edition hardbound copy of *The Feminine Mystique*, and she wanted to enclose a personal note with the book. As she thought about what to write in her note, she might have remembered a conversation she had with her father right before leaving for Smith College in 1938. On that day, Betty vented to her father yet another complaint about her mother's actions. Harry Goldstein silenced his daughter, telling her to stop putting her mother down. Then he said, "Your mother has made it possible for you to have the advantages she didn't have. She couldn't get out of here the way you can now."

Perhaps it was her father's words that prompted Betty Friedan in 1963 to write these words to her mother:

> With all the troubles we have had, you gave me the power to break through the feminine mystique which will not, I think, be a problem any longer for Emily. I hope you accept the book for what it is, an affirmation of the values of your life and mine.

Then she enclosed that note with a copy of the first edition of *The Feminine Mystique* and mailed the package to her mother.

Reluctant Heroines

We who started the [women's movement for equality] were reluctant heroines....We identified, as women, with Everywoman....We came together as crucial molecules, finally reaching a critical mass—catalyzing each other into the actions that became a chain reaction, until the movement of women exploded through all the strata of American society.

Betty Friedan, *It Changed My Life*, 1976

Betty Friedan achieved celebrity status in 1963. By midsummer *The Feminine Mystique* (*TFM*) appeared on best-seller lists. Friedan had successfully promoted her book on television talk shows, had received numerous invitations to lecture, and been featured in the November 1963 issue of *Life* magazine. To manage schedules and contracts for lectures, Friedan hired an agent, instructing him to schedule two-week breaks between lectures so she could spend time with her husband and children. Earnings from lectures and book sales greatly increased Betty's income, money that the Friedans used to pay debts and redecorate their home. Yet Friedan paid a heavy price for her success and notoriety: rejection by her friends and her husband.

As a best-selling author, Friedan had become a "leper in Rockland Country." She and Carl loved to entertain but now nobody wanted to come, nor were they invited to social gatherings. Betty belonged to a carpool with other mothers in Grandview, and they took turns driving their children to various activities. But when her schedule as a best-selling author kept her from meeting her obligations in the carpool, the other mothers, likely jealous of Betty's fame, retaliated by kicking the Friedans out of the carpool. Such rejection caused Betty to remember an earlier time. "I was fourteen in Peoria again," writes Friedan in her memoir, "the girl that didn't get into the sorority because she was Jewish." But this time it was different. She had been banished because she was not only better known than her neighbors but also she had achieved recognition by writing a book that challenged the very texture of the lives of those other drivers in the carpool.

Rejection by her husband was far more painful. Problems between Betty and Carl had started several years back but escalated with the success of *The Feminine Mystique*. Although proud of Betty's success, Carl was jealous of her fame and humiliated when introduced as "Betty's husband" at parties. He retaliated with rude, abusive behaviors at parties and by having affairs with women. His behavior angered and hurt Betty because she felt he had robbed her of a deserved happiness for her achievements.

To help sooth conflicts, the Friedans decided to relocate in New York City in late 1964. Disenchanted with suburbia, they wanted to return to the excitement and intellectual intensity of the city. They purchased a condominium for $17,000 in The Dakota, a legendary older brick building near Central Park. Smaller than the Victorian mansion, their condominium had seven cavernous high-ceilinged rooms with an entry foyer, a dining room, a den, and two bathrooms. Promptly they redecorated. Carl put in bookshelves and Betty picked out deep blue-green tile for the kitchen floors and selected vibrant reds and purples for drapes and upholstery. Together, they arranged to have the walls painted and purchased beautiful old oriental rugs at a second-hand store. To escape the city on holidays and weekends, the Friedans also purchased a summer home on Fire Island in 1965. Their vacation home was a place of happy times for Betty. It was where Emily could ride her bike to her friends' houses, with Mervin, her dog, in the basket; where Danny and Jonathan learned to sail; and where, as a family, they hosted clam chowder parties for friends and neighbors. Their new residences helped Betty and Carl to reconcile their differences, at least for a couple of years.

The change and turmoil that defined Friedan's domestic domain also extended to her professional life: She decided to fire her agent and change publishers. Friedan's frustration with her agent, Marie Rodell, began when she asked her to place excerpts from *TFM* in women's magazines prior to the book's publication. Rodell tried, but editors told her that they thought Friedan's book was an "overstatement," "heavy going," "strident," and too "sociological." Refusing to accept these rejections, Friedan fired Rodell and hired Martha Winston. Enthusiastic about Friedan's book, Winston succeeded in getting excerpts from the first two chapters published in *McCall's* (March 1963) and in the *Ladies' Home Journal* (February 1963).

Betty Friedan's relationship with George Brockway, her editor at W. W. Norton, had also become untenable by late 1963. Friedan was angry that Brockway had only reluctantly invested in promoting and printing more hardbound copies of *TFM*. Brockway was fed up with unrelenting suggestions from Betty and Carl Friedan about how best to promote the book. Editors at Random House contacted Friedan to see if she planned to write another book and if so, did she want to change publishers. She agreed to meet, and in the course of their conversation, she suggested a sequel to *TFM* that explored the texture of the "new life patterns" of those who had moved beyond the feminine mystique. The editors responded with a book contract that included a $30,000 advance to be paid annually in three equal installments.

Friedan selected *Woman: The Fourth Dimension* as the working title for her second book and planned to find examples of the ways that women had applied the "new life patterns" to their lives. In her mind, these new patterns would reveal that women had used the "new life plan" that she had promoted in *TFM*. To make her case, she needed, once again, to interview women. She wanted to talk with a diverse group of women who had read or been exposed to *TFM* and lived in cities and communities throughout the United States. The best opportunity for these meetings would be in conjunction with her frequent speaking engagements. From mid-1963 to mid-1964, Friedan met with countless women in small groups, filling 20 notebooks with notes. Such encounters reassured her that she was on the right track: Most women wanted to gain a greater self-identity and expand their sphere beyond the home. In addition, Friedan also received more than a thousand letters from women who also expressed decisions or desires to change their lives.

In spring 1964, Friedan was given a perfect opportunity to showcase her research. The editors of the *Ladies' Home Journal* (*LHJ*) asked her to edit a special issue that focused on women who had or wanted to move beyond the feminine mystique. Feeling honored and validated, she accepted. With contract in hand, Friedan believed, as editor, that her mandate gave her free reign to shape content and presentation. Thus, from its front cover and advertisements to its articles and fiction, Friedan decided to recruit writers and illustrators who would define, illustrate, and explore the struggles, challenges, and successes of women who had combined their traditional domestic roles with their new self-images as individuals. For the front cover, Friedan proposed an image of a double-headed woman, with a strong woman's face emerging from the face of a pretty, conventional Doris Day–type of housewife, and she decided to use real women instead of models for the fashion pages. As editor, Friedan would write the lead article. To give balance, she asked Alvin Toffler, a social commentator of futurist ideas, to write an article that expressed his reaction when his wife decided to embark on a career. With regard to more practical issues, Friedan commissioned an article on child care used by mothers who worked or had returned to school, and another, "Women and Money," that delineated women's earnings and contributions to the family budget, and if they worked at home. Friedan also wanted to make sure that the fiction reflected new life patterns. Thus she contacted Doris Lessing and Joan Didion, as well as others, to submit short stories because their heroines led lives that were not shaped by relationships with men. Finally, Friedan asked Gwendolyn Brooks, winner of the Pulitzer Prize (1945), to submit a poem about black women.

Then reality set it. Editors of *LHJ* pulled back on their commitment to give Friedan free rein. They accepted her article as well as Toffler's and the one on child care but rejected the article on women and money and all fiction that fell outside their comfort zone of women's femininity. They said "no" to using ordinary women as models for fashions and, at the last minute, they moved Friedan's front-cover image of the double-headed woman to an inside page, substituting it with the "usual pretty women's magazine model on the cover." Finally, the editors refused to print Gwendolyn Brooks's poem, a passionate and angry statement about the plight of black women in American society. Fighting with editors over inclusion of Brooks's poem was Friedan's bitterest battle. Annoyed by Friedan's relentless "stridency" about including the poem, the editors retorted that if she wanted the poem in the magazine, then she could pay them $5,000 and run it as an ad—a challenge she did not take.

Although disappointed with the outcome, Friedan benefited from her experience: She was forced to evaluate her research of new life patterns to write her featured article, "Woman: The Fourth Dimension." With bravado, Friedan begins this article by stating that all "the arguments about the feminine mystique seem obsolete, swept aside by a massive breakthrough in the lives and minds of American women." To support this sweeping statement, she gives examples of women who had moved beyond the feminine mystique. These women, Friedan writes, had stopped defining their lives solely only in terms of a three-dimensional sexual relationship with men as wives, mothers and homemakers and integrated a "fourth dimension" into their existence. Friedan makes clear that the fourth dimension is an added dynamic, not a denial or replacement for the traditional three-dimensional femininity of women as homemakers. She also alerts readers that adding this new dimension is revolutionary—it requires that women "change the way they see themselves and the way others see them." Though she does not laden the narrative with philosophical theories, Friedan warns that those who opt for adding a fourth dimension must be ready to take the existential "leap of faith" into the unknown and must be prepared that defining self-identity is pragmatic—it requires a process of trial and error.

"Woman: The Fourth Dimension" makes a strong case that women had started to move beyond the feminine mystique. But as she reviewed her research, Friedan realized that those that had achieved new life patterns were a small group. Consequently, she was forced to admit that her research revealed that most women were still stuck in a three-dimensional lifestyle. From her reassessment, Friedan came to new conclusions. First, and most promising, the research revealed that many women wanted to add a meaningful, individual pursuit to their three-dimensional separate sphere lifestyles. Second, and more troubling, the research showed that what kept them from moving forward was the absence of essential support services such as quality child care, access to well-paying professional jobs, and availability of part-time degree programs in higher education.

It was this last conclusion—the limited access to essential support systems—that prompted Friedan to shift her research efforts to Washington, D.C. There she would probe and prod to find out whether government officials had considered the needs of women in formulating social policy. And she was hopeful: On July 2, President Lyndon Baines Johnson had signed the Civil Rights Act of 1964, and buried among its amendments was a key phrase that banned sex discrimination in the workplace. Such a phrase, in Friedan's view, could serve as a foundation to wage a campaign for social policies that women needed to achieve a four-dimensional lifestyle and, more importantly, achieve full equality with men in American society.

Just as the Supreme Court's decision on *Brown v. the Board of Education* (1954) initiated the civil rights movement, Title VII of the Civil Rights Act of 1964 was, in Friedan's opinion, "the defining moment that made the women's movement possible." Title VII banned sex and racial discrimination in the workplace, which meant that employers could no longer use gender as a means not to hire or promote women or fire them for getting married or pregnant. Recalling her own hope and enthusiasm, Friedan remembered thinking that women were now "ready to move into the mainstream." Having watched blacks refuse to work or to ride the bus in less than human dignity, women finally could say, "Me, too."

Title VII served as the catalyst for the second wave of feminism by becoming the rallying cry for women who were fed up with their status as second-class citizens. These women, by the early 1960s, had gravitated to three groups, each reflecting a political vantage point. Betty Friedan occupied, and led, those women whose perspective was within the boundaries of political liberalism. As a leader of liberal feminism, Friedan and her constituency demanded aggressive public policies to expand equality and equity to women. By so doing, she and other liberal feminists benefited from the groundswell of social reform emanating from the actions and leadership of Martin Luther King and, by the late 1960s, Cesar Chavez. More importantly, Friedan's political position tapped into a support network of tens of thousands of women who considered political activism for women's rights their pathway of liberating themselves from the feminine mystique.

To Friedan's political right was the traditional agenda of working women. In 1961, John Kennedy had created the President's Commission on the Status of Women (PCSW) giving it the mandate to make recommendations that would end sex discrimination in government and private employment and to identify support services needed by working women who were married and had children. In 1963, the President's Commission published its findings. Using statistics on wages and types of jobs, the report documented that women had lower paid jobs and were promoted less often than men. But the report failed to consider the underlying causes of sex discrimination. For example, the PCSW report endorsed protective legislation for working women without addressing the ways that employers used this policy to keep women in lower paying positions. The commission also opposed the Equal Rights Amendment, a traditional stance of working women since the ERA had been forwarded by Alice Paul in 1923. By so doing, the commission failed to admit that, if passed, the ERA would assure women the right to equal jobs and equal pay.

The report also recommended that the process of gathering statistics on working women be sustained by establishing commissions in each state and creating a permanent citizens' advisory council at the national level. President Kennedy complied. Once 50 state commissions began to investigate and document women's "unequal status," it gave, as Susan Hartmann writes in *From the Margin to the Mainstream: American Women and Politics Since 1960*, "visibility and legitimacy to women's concerns." Moreover, because the women who served in the state commissions gained firsthand exposure to the pervasive reality of women's inequality, they soon became committed activists for women's rights. As activists, these women responded positively to the ideas promoted by Betty Friedan.

To Friedan's political left was a loosely organized collection of women's groups that demanded the end of sexism and the patriarchal system of oppression. Collectively, these groups became identified by 1967 as the women's liberation movement and demographically, most activists were baby boomers. Initially, the women's liberation movement emerged from the New Left student movement of the 1960s which was associated with the Student Nonviolent Coordinating Committee (SNCC), Students for a Democratic Society (SDS), and the anti–Vietnam War movement. As participants in these organizations, these women, like their male counterparts, demanded fundamental changes that would destroy all oppressive institutions in America, from segregation to the draft, and, for some, an end of capitalism.

As part of the radical left, these women believed they would have equal voice and responsibilities in these organizations. They were wrong. Instead, they were assigned "female" roles and treated as sex objects. Such actions caused them to reconfigure their political activism as a personal issue; their mission became a quest to uncover the causes of and remedies for their oppression as women. With its mission to end oppression of women, the women's liberation movement, like a magnet, not only attracted women in the New Left student movement but also other college women, women of color, lesbian feminists, and, by the late 1960s, some of the younger and more progressive members of the National Organization for Women (NOW).

No matter their agendas, the three constituencies of traditional, liberal, and radical women believed they could benefit from the momentum of social reform that dominated domestic politics in the 1960s. Their belief was strengthened by Lyndon Johnson, who won the 1964 presidential election by an overwhelming majority. Johnson decided to use his political mandate to launch the Great Society and the War on Poverty, which he hoped would be his legacy. Central to Johnson's social reform agenda was enforcement of provisions of the Civil Rights Act of 1964. To that end, he established the Equal Employment Opportunity Commission (EEOC) in 1965 to assure compliance with Title VII. In addition, to demonstrate his advocacy for ending sex discrimination in the workplace, Johnson promised to appoint more women to government agency positions, and he demanded that the members of his cabinet find women to promote.

Betty Friedan was not a person who could be content to read about changes for women in the *New York Times*. Because she wanted and needed firsthand accounts, she decided to shift her research efforts to Washington, D.C. Through a series of interviews and observations, she anticipated that she would find actions and policies that led to ending discrimination of women in the workplace and that established pathways for women to move beyond the feminine mystique. She was soon disappointed.

Friedan began by assessing whether Johnson had followed through on his promise to promote women within government agencies. She discovered that he had not appointed a woman to his cabinet or considered nominating a woman for the Supreme Court. Given this, Friedan wanted to find out who had been appointed and what they did. She discovered that most women who had been "promoted" to professional positions in various agencies were merely "tokens." For example, at the State Department, Friedan interviewed a woman whose title was "Assistant-to-the-Assistant Secretary of State," a job that had been newly created. Embittered, this "assistant-to-the-assistant" told Friedan that in her six-month tenure, she had been given only one assignment—to study the department telephone book. While at the State Department, Friedan also asked why young women had not been appointed to the Foreign Service. They, like their male counterparts, had established their credentials by passing the Foreign Service exam. She was told that young women were not typically appointed because if they married, they would be required to resign. When

Friedan asked why, she was told that once married, a woman, who would have access to diplomatic secrets, could no longer be trusted to keep these secrets from her husband. Friedan then asked if the husband would also be required to resign. The answer was no, and the implication was clear: A woman would easily give into pressure and share information, whereas a man was tough enough to keep quiet.

Next, Friedan decided to talk with Sargent Shriver, director of the Office of Economic Opportunity (OEO), the agency that administered the programs for the War on Poverty. Certainly, Friedan reasoned, women would have policy-making positions in this agency because the largest demographic group living in poverty was comprised of women of color and single women with children. She discovered that no woman had a policy-making position at the OEO. Nor were there any programs specific for education programs for women who had dropped out of high school or job-training programs that would give these women well-paying jobs.

Then Friedan turned her attention to the Equal Employment Opportunity Commission (EEOC), the agency that surely would have its finger on the very pulse of sex discrimination in the workplace. President Johnson had appointed five commissioners, four men and one woman, to run the agency. Franklin D. Roosevelt Jr., son of Franklin and Eleanor Roosevelt, served as chair of the EEOC, and among the five commissioners, Richard Graham and Aileen Clarke Hernandez were the only advocates for women's rights. Charged with hiring staff and processing complaints, these five commissioners began operation of the EEOC in July 1965.

The EEOC's mandate was to serve as a clearinghouse that received and processed complaints of race and sex discrimination in the workplace. But the EEOC's leadership directed staff to focus all efforts to processing complaints of discrimination from black men and to ignore complaints submitted by women. Despite this unspoken policy, a third of the complaints submitted to the agency by late 1965 were filed by women in professional and nonprofessional jobs. As one of the agency's commissioners, Aileen Hernandez, a longtime advocate for equal rights for working women, became frustrated by the policy of ignoring claims made by women workers and by the attitudes of the male-dominated commission. She later noted that EEOC meetings typically produced a "sea of male faces, nearly all of which reflected attitudes that ranged from boredom to virulent hostility whenever the issue of sex discrimination was raised."

The EEOC's decision to ignore complaints from women was consistent with the historical assumptions about women workers. Since the early nineteenth century, employers had categorized women as "temporary workers" because they assumed that a woman's lifetime goal was to be a wife and mother. Consequently, women need not be trained for and promoted to higher paying jobs. In addition, employers believed that women were emotionally unable to manage an organization; intellectually unable to comprehend the theories required for professions in science, medicine, and law; and physically unable to work long hours and engage in manual labor. They were the "weaker sex." This historical rationale was the bedrock of complaints submitted to the EEOC by thousands of women in 1965 and 1966. These claims divided into three categories: newspaper help wanted ads that were segregated by sex in separate sections, state protective laws that were used to keep women in lower paying jobs, and bono fide occupational qualifications (BFOQ) that made age, marital status, and gender requirements for employment in specific jobs.

Most pervasive was the impact of newspaper want ads that listed jobs for women and men in two separate sections. Such segregation, one requested by employers, had been the established practice since the 1890s. In the 1960s, this meant a woman who wanted to apply for a job at a bank would discover from the want ads that she could apply as a teller; by contrast, if her brother were looking for a job, he would discover he could apply for bank manager.

Employers also used protective legislation—laws that protected women from undue physical stress in the workplace—to keep women in industry from working overtime and applying for higher paying positions that required physical labor. Until 1970, major labor unions also supported protective legislation because it secured the higher paying jobs for men, the family "breadwinners." State protective legislation laws also significantly diminished the impact of the Equal Pay Act of 1963. Thus employers and male union members benefited from protective legislation because it gave them a rationale to pay women less and to target women workers for layoffs in times of economic recessions.

The concept of BFCQ also kept women in "their place." The employer had the liberty to establish hiring guidelines that not only defined certain jobs as "female only" but also placed restrictions on lifestyles. Friedan had come across an example of this practice when she interviewed women who had passed the Foreign Services exam but were not appointed to the Foreign Service if they were married. A more public example was the claim presented by airline stewardesses. Starting in the 1950s, stewardesses at different major airline companies started fighting to end the airlines' so-called retirement policy. Major airlines had established guidelines that forced female flight attendants to quit at the age of 32 or 35, depending on the airline, or upon marriage. Such guidelines added to profits because the age and marriage requirement meant that the airlines would not be burdened with annual salary increases, higher social security taxes, and increased health care benefits. More covertly, airlines did not hire young women who did not embody the American image of the wholesome "girl next door." Those hired were white, attractive in a feminine, youthful sense, and not overweight. Protests on these guidelines and covert practices began with two American Airlines stewardesses, Nancy Collins and Dusty Roads, in the 1950s. By 1966, there were 92 separate claims by stewardesses among the stack of ignored claims at the EEOC.

When she started probing at the EEOC, Betty Friedan learned from Aileen Hernandez and Richard Graham about the agency's practice to ignore sex discrimination claims. In a conversation with Graham, she learned that he had met with the directors of the League of Women Voters, the American Association of University Women, and other women's organizations with national headquarters in Washington. In these meetings he asked that their organizations pressure the EEOC to enforce the "sex discrimination" clause of Title VII. These leaders were shocked by his request, Graham told Friedan, because they were not "feminists." Friedan also got firsthand information about EEOC's unspoken policy not to process claims on sex discrimination from Sonia Pressman (later Fuentes). In their meeting, Pressman, who had been recently hired and was the only woman on the EEOC's legal team, expressed frustration with the agency's policy on sex discrimination. She also suggested that to effect change, women needed an independent organization that lobbied for their rights.

That the thousands of claims submitted to the EEOC by women workers were ignored also angered women who worked in the Washington bureaucracy, such as Catherine East, a career professional at the Women's Bureau. East was the coordinator of the state commissions that had been established as an outcome of the 1963 report of the President's Commission of the Status of Women (PCSW). As coordinator, East reviewed the state-by-state statistics that documented unequal pay and promotional status of working women. Pauli Murray, a black activist and lawyer who had served on the PCSW, was also upset by the EEOC's noncompliance of Title VII. In December 1965, Murray and Mary Eastwood, a lawyer in the Department of Justice, collaborated on an article, "Jane Crow and the Law." As its title suggests, the piece admonished the nonaction of the EEOC on cases of sex discrimination. A few months earlier, Murray made public these ideas when she spoke at the annual conference of the National Council of Women, held in New York City in October. In her remarks, Murray was blunt, declaring that the EEOC's decision not to process claims on sex discrimination was evidence of a subtle opposition to the "gender clause" of Title VII. Then she challenged listeners to realize that if it "becomes necessary to march on Washington to assure equal job opportunities for all, I hope women will not flinch from the thought."

Friedan read about Murray's speech in the *New York Times*. Immediately she picked up the phone and called her. By the end of their conversation, Friedan realized that both she and Murray had the same goal: immediate enforcement of Title VII for women workers, even if such enforcement required an organization that lobbied for the rights of women. Both women would soon become instrumental in the founding of the National Organization for Women (NOW). In hindsight, Friedan's call to Murray established one of the many historic linkups that led to the second-wave feminist movement.

From her research and new acquaintances, Friedan became increasingly aware that East, Murray, and Pressman were part of a larger network of activists who believed the only way women would gain economic and social equality was if they had an organization that lobbied for their rights, much like the National Association for the Advancement of Colored People (NAACP) had represented African Americans by lobbying for laws and policies to assure their civil rights. Thus East and Murray, as well as others, suggested that Friedan use her influence as a best-selling author to build momentum for founding such an organization. Often, after a day's research in Washington, Friedan met with Catherine East and Mary Eastwood, key members of this network of activists. Over dinner and long into the evening, they talked about the strategies for forming a women's organization and made hypothetical lists of potential members, selecting women who had the know-how and connections to form local chapters of a national organization.

In addition, East and Eastwood told Friedan that they needed to recruit women union workers. To that end, they recommended that Friedan go to Detroit to meet with Dorothy Haener and Caroline Davis, who were union leaders of the United Auto Workers. Haener and Davis organized meetings between Friedan and female workers in the union. At these meetings, she listened as the women told of the unrelenting hassle, the run-around, and the intimidation they faced when they tried to speak up for their rights at union meetings, accounts that might have reminded Friedan of interviews she had had as a labor journalist in the late 1940s.

By early 1966, Friedan had concluded that women needed to establish an organization focused on lobbying for their equal rights. And she intended to be the leader of that organization. The next step was to find out if broad-based support for such an organization existed among women at the local and state levels.

East suggested that women from the state commissions established by the President's Commission on the Status of Women were prime recruits for such an organization. And the timing was right: The third annual meeting of these state commissions was scheduled in Washington, D.C., for June 1966. Attendees at this meeting would be a captive audience, and many were angered by the unequal status of women in the workplace. East secured a guest pass for Friedan so she could attend all the sessions of the three-day meeting. Friedan, in collaboration with East and Pauli Murray, decided they would use this gathering to meet with a handpicked group of women to present their ideas. They scheduled such a meeting in Friedan's hotel room for the evening of the second day. It was a meeting that did not go exactly as Friedan had planned.

East, Murray, and Haener invited key women in the state commissions to this clandestine meeting. Friedan also invited Katherine (Kay) Clarenbach after hearing her "give a biting talk" about the inequality of women. Clarenbach was chair of the Wisconsin Commission on the Status of Women, first president of the Association of State Commissions, and a professor of political science at the University of Wisconsin. That night some fifteen to twenty women assembled in Friedan's room to discuss the feasibility of starting a women's organization. Friedan, Clarenbach, and Murray led the discussion, consistently making the point of the need for such an organization. To some, it seemed that the discussion leaders had already mapped out their plans for an organization and only wanted others to rubber-stamp their plan. For example, one attendee recalled that the acronym of NOW was quickly proposed, and Murray had already outlined an organizational plan on a yellow legal pad.

Feeling pressured, some women at the meeting pulled back, arguing that any advocacy group for women was too risky. Newcomers to the idea of a national women's organization asked what they thought to be appropriate questions, such as "Have we really explored all the alternatives?" Tempers flared as the meeting moved from a preset agenda to a discussion about alternatives. Friedan, characteristically single-minded and aggressive, became visibly annoyed, began to shout, and demanded that naysayers leave. Some refused. Thereafter, any expectations of gaining unanimous support for founding a women's organization at this latenight meeting were lost. Instead after angry outbursts subsided, the group decided to present two resolutions that validated their collective concerns. The first resolution called for the enforcement of Title VII by the EEOC on cases of sex discrimination, and the second called for the reappointment of Richard Graham, advocate of women's rights, to the EEOC. Clarenbach was chosen to give these two resolutions to the conference leaders so they could submit them to a vote of the general membership. Once everyone left, Friedan went to bed feeling the bitter taste of defeat.

In the morning session, the officials of the conference, worried about the political fallout of pressuring the Johnson administration, refused to put to a vote the two resolutions forwarded by Clarenbach. Friedan and other militants, angered by this action, shifted to more aggressive tactics. Hastily, they decided to sit together at two adjacent tables at lunch to plan their next move. In conspiratorial fashion, they whispered, passed around notes on paper napkins, and again discussed forming a new organization.

After lunch, 28 women gathered in a small meeting room for about an hour to set up a temporary organization. Decisions at this meeting included agreement on the organization's name, the National Organization for Women (NOW), and its central objective: to "bring women into full participation in the mainstream of American society and in truly equal partnership with men." In addition, the group selected Clarenbach as temporary chairperson, and in that role she would select an executive committee to assist her. Monthly membership dues were set at $5. This meeting was transformational for Gene Boyer, a woman from Beaver Dam, Wisconsin. When she learned that NOW would rely on local chapters, she wanted to be a charter member. Boyer, like many, was aware of the "undiscovered hordes of frustrated feminists buried alive in the small, dusty corners of the nation." NOW became even a greater reality to Boyer when another woman at the organizational meeting pulled out a five-dollar bill from her wallet and "invited" others to put their money down and sign their names. Boyer left to catch her plane to Wisconsin, believing she and the others at that meeting had participated in a significant beginning.

Betty Friedan might not have left this meeting with the same enthusiasm. She must have felt outmaneuvered because she was not appointed to a specific leadership role. Clarenbach, not she, was selected to act as "temporary chair," and Clarenbach, not she, would select members of the executive committee. Friedan worried that the gravitational force of this nascent organization for women had moved away from her and the Washington network of activists to Clarenbach's power base in the Midwest. With this shift, Friedan's desire to lead NOW seemed uncertain.

Within a week, Clarenbach had selected the temporary steering committee to organize NOW—and Friedan was not on it. Pauli Murray was the only member appointed to this committee from Friedan's power base. Clarenbach's selections implied that she envisioned a women's organization focused on advancing the agendas of the State Commissions on the Status of Women and centered in the Midwest. Equally, she and others on the hand-picked steering committee wanted to minimize Friedan's role because they feared her avowed feminist position and flamboyant, combative personal style might keep many women from joining NOW.

By mid-July, Friedan realized she had been shut out by Clarenbach, and she was hurt, angry, and concerned. Personally, she felt entitled to be the leader of NOW because, in her mind, she had been preselected as its standard-bearer by those working at the EEOC and other government agencies. In addition, she believed the agenda, tactics, and strategies of NOW needed to be public and militant; otherwise, like so many women's organizations, it would not effect significant change. Third, Friedan knew it was she, not Clarenbach, who was already a public figure and whose name had the national recognition that would be critical to attract media attention. Finally, Friedan realized she could attract future members to NOW from the built-in constituency of the hundreds of thousands of women who had read *The Feminine Mystique*, flocked to hear her impassioned speeches, and expressed that they were ready to agitate and protest for equal rights.

To deal with the looming possibility of "a takeover" by the Midwestern faction, Friedan asked East and Eastwood to come to her summer home at Fire Island for a strategy session. The first day, the three women vented their anger. Then the trio began to figure out how to rectify some of the decisions and directions that Clarenbach had put into place. They focused on three issues: First, the official "launching" of NOW must be either in New York or Washington, D.C., because the event would gain greater attention by the media. Second, recruitment of charter members must include women who were aggressive in their tactics and lived in major urban areas such as New York City. Third, Friedan should be given a policy-making position in NOW and write the organization's "Statement of Purpose." Then Friedan called Clarenbach.

Although Friedan never documented the tone and contents of this conversation, it must have been tense. Yet Clarenbach realized the merit of Friedan's points and agreed. Most significant to the early success of NOW, the two women, who likely would have otherwise never collaborated, decided to divide the leadership of NOW. Friedan would be president and Clarenbach, chair of the board. Friedan would use her national reputation and flamboyant style to gain media attention, her ability as a writer to promote the agenda of NOW, and her genius for envisioning NOW as an all-encompassing organization that reached out to women of all ages and economic circumstances. Clarenbach could use her expertise, patience, and support network to attend to the essential procedures it took to build an organization, and she could attract a significant number of members to NOW from the Midwest. Truly, as noted in *The Feminist Chronicles*, the "division at that time of the top leadership" between Clarenbach and Friedan was "clearly an astute stroke."

October 29, 1966 marks the "official founding" of the National Organization for Women—the first new feminist organization in nearly 50 years. Thirty-two of the 300 charter members gathered in the John Philip Sousa Room of the *Washington Post* in the nation's capital. Betty Friedan was there, but Kay Clarenbach was not. The group first voted on the slate of officers. In addition to Friedan and Clarenbach, these included Aileen Hernandez, as executive vice president; Richard Graham, vice president; and

Caroline Davis, secretary treasurer. After electing officers, the group turned its attention to approving the organization's "Statement of Purpose" (see Appendix A). Friedan had spent the summer months writing this document, a process that included close collaboration with Pauli Murray.

In drafting the "Statement of Purpose," Betty Friedan, in many ways, articulated her own concept of feminism. What she advocates in this document, as well as in her actions in the second wave of feminism, is a "true gender democracy." To achieve this gender democracy, she calls for a recasting of traditional gender roles within marriage that would create a "true partnership," in which husband and wife would equally share the responsibilities of home and the economic burden of their support. At the same time, the federal and state governments must participate in this expansion of democracy by establishing and funding support services such as health care, child care, and pregnancy leave.

What is more significant about the "Statement of Purpose" is its scope. It extends its concerns beyond the narrow segment of middle- and upper-class, college-educated, largely suburban women with whom Friedan had been concerned in *The Feminine Mystique*. It cites the unequal status of women in the workplace as a means to make an argument for aggressive action and change. Reflective of Friedan's evocative writing style, the statement tells of a passionate concern for "the worldwide revolution of human rights now taking place within and beyond our national borders," and it points out that black women are "the victims of the double discrimination of race and sex," illustrated by the reality that two-thirds were employed "in the lowest paid service occupations." Next, displaying her long-standing political positions of social justice and progressive ideas, Friedan makes clear that gender equality and equity must be part of a nation that stands on the principle that "human rights for all are indivisible" and that has pledged "to give active support to the common cause of equal rights for all those who suffer discrimination and deprivation."

As one looks back, the decisions made in that October 1966 meeting of NOW have had a positive impact on the lives of women and men in American society. Yet the first meeting of NOW barely registered in the national consciousness. The *Washington Post* placed their story, "Neo-Suffragettes on the March: Mrs. Friedan Is Fighting for Women's Equality NOW," next to an ad for a "fashion clearance" and below photographs of diplomatic wives greeting each other. The *New York Times* placed its story, "They Meet in a Victorian Parlor to Demand 'True Equality,'" beneath recipes for turkey and stuffing.

"The founding of a feminist civil rights organization of some sort," notes historian Ruth Rosen, "was probably inevitable" because women needed a nongovernmental organization that "could pressure the government from the outside." But at the time, it was seen as "an audacious act" that frightened potential members. Women who joined NOW in its early years, notes Rosen, publicly acknowledged "that liberal political culture was inadequate to address the reality of women's lives." Friedan would agree. In her view, NOW changed the configuration of problems and solutions. Once women "dared to judge" their conditions as women "by the simple standard, the hallmark of American democracy—equality, no more, no less," then "separate but equal" was out of the question. Thereafter, feminists redefined equality and liberty for modern women which turned "the entire culture upside down."

Shortly before the small group of charter members adjourned in October 1966, they shared, as Friedan has written, "a moving moment of realization" that they had "indeed entered history." This epiphany was prompted by Murray. She passed around a medallion that she had been given by one of the survivors of the battle for the women's vote in America some 50 years earlier. She told the group that this medallion had belonged to a woman who had been imprisoned and had tried to starve herself in protest in a jail near where the charter members were meeting. Then Alice Rossi, also a charter member at the meeting, recalled that "exactly one hundred years ago two British women took the first petition for the vote for women to the British Parliament—and did not know how to get it inside except by hiding it in the bottom of a cart of apples being taken for the members to eat." Then, as Friedan writes, "We suddenly realized the confidence and courage we must share—to confront the complex unfinished business of the revolution they started so long ago, to launch this new movement for full equality for all women in America, in truly equal partnership with men."

Then Betty Friedan and others left for home, all deeply committed to engage in the Unfinished Revolution for Everywoman.

The Unfinished Revolution

If anything were to be said about me when the history of the movement is written, I'd like it to read, "She was the one who said women were people, she organized them and taught them to spell their own names."

Betty Friedan, Interview, 1970

Borrowing from James Baldwin's claim that the black man would never be free until he could learn to spell his own name, Betty Friedan believed that until women learned to spell out their own needs, they would never realize equal status in society. Friedan contributed the necessary tools: By articulating the undefined grievances of suburban housewives in *The Feminine Mystique*, she provided an alphabet that women used to spell out their needs. By leading the National Organization for Women in its early and most fragile years, she gave them the necessary paper and pencil.

Friedan left the first meeting of NOW ready to lead the unfinished revolution that would "bring women into full participation in the mainstream of American society." She was excited and ready to channel her considerable energy and influence into making sure that this revolution succeeded. Initially, NOW stumbled along as competing constituencies debated about issues, distribution of responsibilities, and appropriate tactics and strategies. What kept these competing voices from destroying NOW was the strong and uncompromising presence of Betty Friedan. One activist reported that Friedan's greatest strength—her aggressiveness—was needed for two reasons. First, Friedan dominated executive board meetings so that NOW could stay focused on actions that affected change. Second, Friedan's popularity and charisma as a speaker at college campuses, community groups, and various conferences inspired listeners to start local chapters of NOW.

In its first year, NOW was its most vulnerable. It had only 300 charter members and no money, staff, or central office. Therefore, the responsibilities for this fledgling organization were distributed among the leadership. As president, Friedan held policy meetings at her home in New York City; as chair of the board, Clarenbach used her faculty office at the University of Wisconsin to generate board policies and minutes; and as secretary-treasurer, Caroline Davis, a member of the United Auto Workers, used union facilities to print, mail, and keep membership records. Muriel Fox, founder of the New York City chapter of NOW, used her position in a leading public relations firm to publicize actions of the organization. Though fragmented in its organizational structure, NOW had a successful first year, much to the credit of Friedan.

As primary architect, Friedan realized that the immediate actions needed to be focused. Therefore, in many late-night policy meetings, Friedan and her inner circle decided to make sex discrimination in the workplace their one-issue agenda because this issue had the broad-based support from existing and potential members of NOW. These strategy sessions led to offensives on several fronts. The first volley targeted the Equal Employment Opportunity Commission (EEOC). NOW pressured the commission to initiate public hearings on its advertising guidelines on sex-segregated want ads; it threatened legal action if the commission did not enforce the prohibition of sex discrimination; and it demanded that the agency appoint women as commissioners and hire women for policy-making positions. The second volley landed in the Oval Office of the White House: NOW pressured

President Johnson to extend affirmative action to hiring practices for women. In 1965, Johnson had issued an executive order that prohibited discrimination by race in hiring practices of companies doing business with the federal government; NOW reasoned that women deserved equal treatment. The third line of attack was to provide legal expertise and support to the claims made by airline stewardesses who were required to quit when they turned 35, and to women workers whose prospects for overtime and promotion were derailed by state protective legislation laws.

NOW's final attack was to gain public attention and support. In August 1967, members of the New York chapter of NOW picketed the *New York Times* to protest the sex segregation of advertising for employment. To assure media attention, protesters dressed in old-fashioned costumes to emphasize the "old-fashioned policies" of the newspaper. As a ploy for media attention, the protest was a success. It was featured in the nightly news shows and reported, complete with a photograph, in the *Times*. In December, NOW declared a National Day of Demonstration against the EEOC and mobilized women to picket local EEOC offices. In New York City, Washington, D.C., Pittsburgh, San Francisco, Chicago, and Atlanta, protestors brought bundles of newspapers tied with red ribbon tape and dumped them "at the government's feet." In New York, NOW members emblazoned the bundles with "Title Seven Has No Teeth; EEOC Has No Guts." Skilled at "making a fuss," the women, once again, tipped off the local television stations so their actions made the evening news.

The impact of NOW's war on sex discrimination went beyond attracting the attention of the media. The most significant first-year victory was action by President Lyndon Johnson. In October 1967, Johnson signed Executive Order 11375, which prohibited sex discrimination in employment by the federal government and by contractors doing business with the government. The results were far reaching: Any university or company that received federal contracts now had to ensure fair employment to women as well as to racial minorities. That same year, the National Federation of Business and Professional Women's Clubs, with a membership of 170,000, cited state protective labor laws as the major cause of both direct and indirect discrimination against women in many fields. Such a stance by this group showed that other organizations had heard NOW's message. Other victories were to follow: In August 1968, the EEOC banned segregated want ads, an action directly attributable to NOW's lobbying efforts and protests. With the added legal advice and public support of NOW, airline stewardesses succeeded in their 1968 court case in removing age and marriage requirements as guidelines for employment. And by 1969, women workers who had been restricted by state protective legislation laws from applying for physically taxing (and higher paying) jobs won civil action suits, specifically because of NOW's public advocacy and the expertise and moneys from its Legal Defense and Education Fund.

Based on early victories and pending actions, Betty Friedan knew that her strategy to make sex discrimination the vehicle to establish NOW had worked. Thus she used this successful strategy as her bully pulpit at the first annual meeting of NOW, held in Washington, D.C., on November 17 and 18. At this meeting, Friedan bragged, as well as congratulated, NOW members. "In this incredibly fast-paced year," she began, "we have been so busy organizing and acting on behalf of [women's] full equality—and so harassed by the day-to-day-problems involved, with no resources but our own energy, persistence, and dedication—that we are hardly aware of how far we have come." Then she offered markers to measure this distance. In one year, members of NOW had quadrupled from 300 to more than 1,200 women and men. Dramatic increases in membership reflected that local chapters were being organized "almost weekly" in California, Illinois, Wisconsin, Ohio, New England, Pennsylvania, New York, the nation's capital, and the southern states. But a more significant marker, in Friedan's opinion, was the proactive, impatient, and dedicated mind-set of its members; it was their "seriousness, perseverance, ingenuity, and indeed, elegance" that had created "the image of women which America sorely needs."

Friedan then gave concrete examples of the ways that individual members and organized efforts in local chapters had made significant gains in ending sex discrimination in the workplace. In recalling these examples, she made clear that she had been proven right: Making sex discrimination the focal point of NOW's first year had given this infant organization the necessary visibility and credibility. But even though attacking sex discrimination had been a successful first step, Friedan argued that it was not an issue that could sustain the longer, more difficult journey that would lead to women's equal status in American society, politics, and economics. Such a journey required calling for revolutionary change. To that end, Betty Friedan called on NOW's members to wage a battle in this unfinished revolution. For this fight, she proposed a battle plan—the Bill of Rights for Women (see Appendix B).

Conceived and written by Friedan, the Bill of Rights for Women lists eight demands that range from mainstream to revolutionary. Positioned in mainstream reform, this document calls for enforcement of affirmative action for women in the workplace and additional legislation that assures equal access to admission and funding for higher education. More progressive, it advocates expanding federally funded social welfare programs to include paid maternity leave, child-care facilities, and funds for job training, housing, health care, and living expenses for women in poverty. Most revolutionary, the Bill of Rights for Women demands that women have access to legal abortion on demand and that the Equal Rights Amendment (ERA) be added to the U.S. Constitution. Legal abortion and the ERA were, for Friedan, the "gut issues." Without them, women would never have a "real security—and equality and human dignity—whether they worked outside or inside the home." She also realized that not all members of NOW would support the inclusion of these two revolutionary demands.

The demand for legal abortion alienated existing as well as potential members who opposed abortion on religious grounds. As a consequence, Catholic nuns, some of whom were on NOW's Executive Board, and other "pro-life" members resigned. These individuals, however, did not abandon the women's rights movement. They founded the Women's Equity Action League (WEAL), so they could join NOW on lobbying for an end to sexual discrimination in employment and an equal rights amendment.

The demand for the ERA meant that those who belonged to labor unions would resign from NOW. Historically, the official policy of labor unions was not to support the ERA because it would negate protective legislation laws, which labor unions supported. One of the greatest losses was Caroline Davis, who, as a member of United Auto Workers (UAW), had to resign as secretary-treasurer of NOW. However, the loss of Davis and other union members was short lived: In 1970, the year the ERA was reintroduced in the U.S. Congress, major unions, including the UAW, decided to support the amendment.

Betty Friedan's decision to include the demand for the ERA led to one of the high points of the first annual meeting of NOW. After she had presented the Bill of Rights, she opened up the meeting for discussion. During that discussion, some of the "very old suffragists," women who had fought for the Nineteenth Amendment and had supported an Equal Rights Amendment since the 1920s, spoke about their experiences. Their presence and comments, as Friedan remembers, "spoke to those very young women who had never heard before about their struggles." The suffragists inspired these new activists, making them aware that sexual discrimination went deeper than "narrow job issues."

Equally inspired, Friedan told members that it was now their "responsibility to history, to take the torch of equality from those tired, valiant women who'd grown old, lonely, keeping it alive." They, as members of NOW, needed to take on this responsibility not only out of allegiance to the activists of the past, but also for the young women in the future who would "take that torch from us." Members of NOW honored their foremothers on Mother's Day 1968. They demonstrated in front of the White House at the same place where the suffragists had protested some 50 years earlier. Friedan and others brandished posters, "Rights Not Roses," and dumped aprons in a huge trash pile. Congress also honored these suffragists by voting in favor of the ERA in 1972.

NOW officially sanctioned and published its Bill of Rights for Women in early 1968. Most immediately, its list of demands clearly repositioned NOW as an organization that advocated revolutionary changes in the ways that American social, political, and economic institutions treated women. Thus, by getting the Bill of Rights for Women as a plan of action, Friedan took control and pushed NOW's gravitational force to the liberal left. Equally important, this plan of action gave Friedan and other leaders of NOW a set of clearly defined objectives that helped recruit new members, take public stands, shape ongoing protests, and add muscle to lobbying efforts.

Despite her success, Friedan soon discovered that her campaign for fighting the unfinished revolution for women's equality and equity was not the only battle being waged. Those who had become part of the women's liberation movement also wanted a revolution, one far more radical. Specifically, radical feminists, as disenchanted veterans of the New Left, had, by the late 1960s, refocused their activism to liberate women from the pervasive impact of sexual politics, a theory that asserts politics and culture are male dominated and male defined and that considers women inferior and subordinate. Sexual politics stands on the twin pillars of sexism and patriarchy. Sexism assumes that men are more valuable members of society than women. As such, they, as patriarchs, are better qualified than women to structure the practices in the family and government, in religion and education, and in economics and education. As a consequence, sexism and patriarchy dictated that women, as individuals and collectively, were required to assume a secondary, subordinate place in which they would depend on men and define themselves in relation to men. Such second-tier status was a causative factor, according to feminists, to a woman's poor self-image and low self-confidence. Such oppression must end.

Feminists in the women's liberation movement realized that before women could take actions to end their oppression, they first needed to understand that sexual politics shaped their personal lives in the kitchen, bedroom, nursery, and their public lives in the media, the classroom, and the workplace. To confront their experiences required "consciousness-raising." Created and defined by radical feminists, consciousness-raising was a process by which women in small groups explored the political aspects of their personal life. In these groups, women were encouraged to share experiences by answering questions about their lives. Common questions were "Discuss your relationships with men. Have you noticed any recurring patterns?" "Discuss your relationships with other women. Do you compete with women for men?" "Growing up as a girl, were you treated differently from your brother?"

By sharing life stories and questioning the so-called natural order of things, women began to see their condition through their own eyes. This clarity of vision enabled them to reflect on the choices they had made and, more importantly, on how others had encouraged and discouraged their decisions. They then realized that the obstacles and constraints they experienced were not caused by their "female" temperament or their lack of talent and intelligence.

Many feminists wrote about the impact of consciousness-raising. For example, Jo Freeman, who cofounded the Chicago chapter of NOW in 1968, discovered that personal problems were "common problems" that had "social causes and political solutions." Susan Brownmiller, who joined the New York Radical Women in 1968, remembered consciousness-raising as a process in which "a woman's experience at the hands of men was analyzed as a *political* phenomenon." Like Freeman and Brownmiller, other women discovered that their experiences of oppression had deeper cultural, social, and economic causes. Their personal experiences were rooted in the political society created and run by men: Therefore, the personal is political.

As a structureless phenomenon, women's liberation groups used various approaches to combat oppression of sexism. Some attempted to transform relations with men; others argued that heterosexual relationships locked women into second-class status. In addition, not all liberation groups espoused radical politics. Although some sustained their involvement with the New Left, others discarded political radicalism. Divisions along sexual stances and politics did not hamper the growth of the women's liberation movement, however. Between 1968 and 1970, feminist discussion groups splintered and multiplied, permeating city, campus, and suburb. Women's liberation "was not a movement; it's a State of Mind," one feminist told a reporter for the *New York Times* in 1970.

Friedan gave little credibility to claims made by women's liberation groups about sexual politics, and she did not agree that consciousness-raising would be the catalyst that ended women's inequality. Instead, she held her ground, arguing that women and men must work together to reconfigure their relationships with one another. Teamwork, not consciousness-raising, would enable women and men to realize that men were fellow victims in women's "half-equality." Such insight would give women the confidence to demand their rightful equality in the public sphere and would persuade men to assume equal responsibility in the private sphere.

The power of her rhetoric and logic made Friedan's approach appealing to her power base of middle-class married women who lived in suburban communities. However, her vision for women's full equality with men was myopic—it saw only one road to success, the one paved by her own agenda. As a consequence, she attacked liberation feminists in speeches, interviews, and articles. Those who engaged in consciousness-raising as a way to realize their oppression were, in Friedan's view, "navel gazing" and "man-hating" individuals who made men the enemy both inside and outside the bedroom and liked to "wallow around in self-pity."

Equally, Betty Friedan, as president of NOW, opposed public support by NOW for the rights of lesbians, which she made clear by excluding their rights from the Bill of Rights for Women. She, along with others on the executive board, believed that if NOW, in its first years, supported lesbian rights, it would likely be perceived as "anti-male." Friedan saw the potential negative fallout in three areas. First, she reasoned that if NOW, in its infancy, was to become aligned with gay rights, it would lose potential members from its power base of heterosexual middle-class women. Friedan's "own position, from the beginning," writes Marilyn French, "had been to gain rights for women without alienating men" because they were "fellow victims of a divisive, repressive, dehumanized society." Second, including support for lesbian rights would lead to its members being tarred, as their suffragist foremothers had been, with being abnormal, too "mannish." As Shelia Tobias observes in *Faces of Feminism*, "Friedan knew history: how lesbianism had to remain hidden through so much of America's past and how much and how often America's suffragist forebears—indeed, any American woman who chose to be outspoken and nontraditional—had to defend herself against sexual innuendo." Third, Betty Friedan had a different vision for

NOW: It was to be an organization that would use its political clout to argue for programs and laws that enabled women to combine their domestic roles as wives and mothers with their aspirations to pursue meaningful work and/or activities in the public sphere. Determined and single-minded, Friedan did not want to clutter up her vision for women's equality with the rights of lesbians. In the women's movement, liberation was about equality not lesbianism.

Certainly Betty Friedan's stance, in hindsight, was short-sighted. She had, as she later admitted, her own "hang-ups" about homosexuality, and she defined her own sexuality in terms of her sexual intimacy with men. Unfortunately, this bias kept her from making the distinction between her personal attitudes about sexuality and her public responsibility to respect the attitudes of homosexual and bisexual women, most especially those who joined NOW. For example, in 1969, Rita Mae Brown, a lesbian feminist and member of the New York City chapter of NOW, demanded to know why issues related to lesbianism were never raised at NOW meetings. Her question was met with "stony silence." Brown's query caused Friedan to warn the members of the national executive board about the "dangers" of linking lesbian feminism to NOW. In response, Brown and two others resigned. A year later, Del Martin, a founder of the lesbian organization Daughters of Bilitis and secretary of the NOW chapter in San Francisco, wrote Friedan in 1970, asking that NOW take a stand in support of lesbian rights. Friedan never replied. Brown responded by leaving NOW. She joined Redstockings, a radical women's liberation group, and later she cofounded Radicalesbians. When Dolores Alexander, NOW's National Executive Director, tried to persuade Friedan to incorporate certain lesbian stands into NOW, she responded by having Alexander fired. Not deterred by Friedan's belligerency, lesbians and lesbian supporters in NOW's New York City chapter decided to take control by running for office. Because this lesbian slate of candidates might win, Friedan packed the meeting with her allies, as well as attending herself. As a consequence, Friedan's slate of candidates won an easy victory over the lesbian candidates.

Friedan's anti-lesbian intolerant actions had consequences. Like Martin, many lesbians and lesbian supporters left NOW and joined various groups in the women's liberation movement. In addition, Friedan's actions caused lesbians and lesbian supporters in NOW to rally support within the organization. At NOW's National Convention in 1970, lesbians and their supporters presented the Constitution of Lesbian Feminist Liberation and demanded that their constitution be incorporated as an addendum into NOW's Statement of Purpose. Writers of this manifesto used Friedan's Bill of Rights for Women as its punching bag by systematically detailing the ways that NOW had refused to extend these rights to lesbians. The majority of attendees voted for the manifesto, thereby making lesbian rights part of the official agenda of NOW.

That vote stands as a repudiation of Friedan's anti-lesbian stance and behavior. More significantly, the Constitution on Lesbian Feminist Liberation affirms that NOW recognized the "double oppression of women who are lesbians"; resolved "that a woman's right to her own person includes the right to define and express her own sexuality and to choose her own lifestyle"; and acknowledged "the oppression of lesbians as a legitimate concern of feminism." Unfortunately, it took Betty Friedan another seven years and more tirades against the "Lavender Menace" to make a public statement that affirmed these inalienable rights for lesbians.

Battling the "radical fringe" of the second-wave feminist movement was not the only battle in Friedan's life in the late 1960s: Her personal life was falling apart. By 1969, she had reached an impasse. Her formula for personal happiness and fulfillment no longer worked. As a high school senior, she had structured for herself an equation:

Husband + children + an absorbing interest for success and fame = personal happiness and self-fulfillment

Since that time, she thought she had put into place these essential factors. In 1947, she fell in love with and married Carl Friedan; she was the mother of three healthy and bright children;

she wrote *The Feminine Mystique* and was a founder and the president of NOW. Yet, Friedan found herself haggling with her husband over the financial arrangements in a pending divorce, watching her adolescent children make plans for college and their independent lives as adults, and experiencing her imploding credibility to lead the unfinished revolution for women.

Betty and Carl Friedan had always had problems. Their long-standing conflicts over money, Carl's sexual liaisons, and Betty's messy, disorganized, and nonattentive approach to housekeeping escalated in the 1960s to a seething, explosive, unpredictable violent rage. In their messy and expensive legal proceedings, each accused the other of verbal and physical abuses. After considerable haggling about details, Carl and Betty Friedan settled on a financial arrangement for their divorce. They sold their condominium in New York City and their summer home at Fire Island and split the profits equally. Carl agreed to pay child support and college tuition, and Betty did not ask for alimony. After the condominium sold, Betty sublet a four-bedroom duplex near Central Park. Emily, age 13, and Jonathan, age 17, lived with her; Daniel, age 21, was at Princeton University.

On May 14, 1969, after giving a lecture on the women's movement at the Episcopal Cathedral in Jackson, Mississippi, Betty flew to Chihuahua, Mexico, not for a vacation but to get a "quick divorce." After going through the legal process that ended her 22-year marriage, Betty adjourned to a bar, ordered a drink, and cried for "all those wasted years." She also cried because she, at 48, feared that she'd never again have a loving, meaningful relationship. Equally, she could not have helped noting the irony of her new status: As author of *The Feminine Mystique*, she would no longer be seen as a woman who had successfully combined her feminine role as wife and mother and her personal aspiration for a meaningful career. Or, that she, as a founder of NOW, could no longer serve as model to those who supported an agenda for bringing "true equality for all women in America" in a full equal partnership with men. That day Friedan cried because *The Feminine Mystique* had dealt a mortal blow to her marriage and the National Organization for Women had dug its grave.

Another reason that Friedan might have found herself crying in a bar in Mexico was that she, as president of NOW, was losing her credibility among members. Her aggressive, self-centered, and combative style had offended many who worked with her. One coworker stated that Friedan was "a terror to deal with" and she had "an overpowering ego at work." She became infamous for calling associates late at night, demanding that they type and mimeograph a press release, speech, or memo, and, if they declined, she would launch into abusive tirades. In addition, board members of NOW objected to her lack of organizational skills. Friedan never learned to chair a meeting, having little patience for Robert's Rules of Order, and she was not interested in the mundane chores of organizing.

More damaging to her reputation as a leader was the fact that Friedan, focused on her own agenda, alienated the younger, more radical members of NOW as well as those associated with the women's liberation movement, and she had systematically purged lesbian feminists and their supporters from NOW. Radical and lesbian feminists considered Friedan an albatross that they wanted to shed. A member of the New York Radical Feminist organization stated that Friedan "misrepresents the case for feminism by making people believe that reform is the answer" when, in fact, the "problem is more fundamental, the entire society has to be upended."

By 1970, members of NOW's Executive Board decided to list Aileen Hernandez as their choice as president, and members of NOW would vote for candidates at the national meeting to be held in Chicago. Hernandez had served as NOW's executive vice president since 1966 and was less combative than Friedan. More significantly, Hernandez could broaden the reach of NOW because she was an African American civil rights and feminist activist and had an established track record as an advocate for increasing programs and opportunities for women living in poverty. At the same time, the board members wanted to keep Friedan a part of the national organization because she had significant supporters within NOW and the power to attract new members. To achieve this objective, they created a National Advisory Board and named her as its chair.

Betty Friedan did not give up her role as president quietly. At the national meeting she gave a two-hour farewell address, ending it by stating "I have led you into history; I leave you now—to make new history." A bold statement that gave her a standing ovation but a statement that was not quite accurate: Friedan was not ready to relinquish her position of leading women to make new history. At a press conference to announce Hernandez as the new president, Friedan made an announcement of her own: Without consulting Hernandez or any newly elected national officers, she proposed that NOW organize the Women's Strike for Equality on August 26, 1970. The date for the 24-hour strike was strategic: It marked the 50th anniversary of the passage of the Nineteenth Amendment. At this press conference, Friedan promoted her idea by challenging NOW members to accept "the responsibility of mobilizing the chain reaction we have helped release, for an instant revolution against sexual oppression in this year, 1970." The August 26 strike would demonstrate "a resistance both passive and active, of all women in America against the concrete conditions of their oppression." Visionary in concept and inspiring in rhetoric, Friedan called on women to use their "power to declare an ultimatum" on all who had kept them from using their rights as Americans. She proposed that secretaries cover their typewriters and close their notebooks, telephone operators unplug their switchboards, waitresses stop serving, cleaning women stop cleaning, and that "everyone who is doing a job for which a man would be paid more—stop—every woman pegged forever as assistant, doing jobs for which men get credit—stop." Then, as dusk fell that day, "instead of cooking dinner or making love, we will assemble, and we will carry candles symbolic of that flame of the passionate journey down through history—relit anew in every city—to converge the visible power of women at city hall—at the political arena where the larger options of our life are decided. And by the time these twenty-four hours are ended, our revolution will be a fact."

Friedan's evocative words rallied supporters and her decision to make the idea public without consulting Hernandez gave her the sole responsibility for organizing the event—which was her objective. As the leader of the strike coalition, she could validate that she was still a leader in the second-wave feminist movement, and it would give her a forum to promote her agenda for women's full equality. What prompted Friedan to call for a nationwide protest, however, was far greater than her ego. Deeply troubled by the cacophony among feminist groups, Friedan wanted to find some action that struck a harmonious chord between mainstream and radical feminists, and she wanted to convince critics that women's rights were to be taken seriously. The Women's Strike for Equality, she believed, would refocus activists to get the women's movement "back on the right path, toward a positive end toward full equality instead of one that fed the fires of impotent rage."

As she faced the monumental task of organizing a nationwide strike in less than five months, Friedan had to make decisions. First, she needed to reposition the Strike for Equality from a 24-hour national event to a series of rallies and demonstrations organized by local chapters of NOW in major cities and small communities across the nation. Second, to prove that mainstream and radical feminist groups could find common ground, Friedan focused the Strike for Equality on three central demands that all feminists wanted: abortion on demand and an end to forced sterilization; free 24-hour child-care centers; and equal opportunity in jobs and education. Third, throughout the five months of preparations for strike day, Friedan applied her heavy-handed, aggressive management style to assure that the Strike for Equality stayed focused on its objective to unify liberal and radical feminists.

Friedan's iron hand was most obvious in organizing the event in New York City, which was slated to be the focal point for the national event. And her battles with radical feminists were formidable. Feminists of the Youth Socialist Alliance, for example, fought with Friedan about the parade route and tactics. Because they believed that total revolution was the only solution to women's rights, these radicals wanted to use the strike in New York as a venue for massive confrontations and street theater. Friedan derailed the radicals' plan by bulldozing her agenda forward. She succeeded in forging a coalition with radical feminist groups because they found the idea of a massive demonstration irresistible. These groups also realized Friedan's power. As radical feminist Susan Brownmiller observed, "If any other woman had called a strike press conference, she would have been talking to herself. Without the name of Betty Friedan, the strike would never have happened."

As a warm-up act to Strike Day, NOW members "liberated" the Statue of Liberty on August 10 by brandishing a banner at the site: "Women of the World Unite!" Nelson Rockefeller, governor of New York, followed when he honored Betty Friedan along with Susan B. Anthony and Elizabeth Cady in a speech at Seneca Falls on August 26. That same day there were demonstrations and rallies in more than ninety major cities and small towns in 42 states—and all had been organized by local NOW chapters. But it was in the streets of New York City that the Strike for Equality gave the women's movement a new dignity.

The morning of the strike, Betty Friedan decided to wear a raspberry dress that she had bought in a recent trip to Finland and to have her hair done at Vidal Sassoon, an upscale trendy hair salon. When asked by reporters, who followed her throughout the day, why she, as a feminist, had her hair done, she quipped, "I don't want people to think Women's Lib girls don't care about how they look. We should try to be as pretty as we can. It's good for our self-image and it's good for politics." Then she joined her "NOW sisters" on Wall Street where they had spent the morning protesting the absence of women in the Stock Exchange and by eating lunch at a venerable "men's-only" restaurant. Then in midafternoon, she took a bus to the entrance of Central Park where marchers were told to assemble. As she walked from the bus stop to the park entrance, Friedan prepared herself for a small turnout. But her fears quickly evaporated. Before her were some 50,000 women and men ready to march.

Friedan took the lead and the march began. In the front row, she walked between a veteran suffragist in her 80s, who had marched the same route in 1920, and a young radical in blue jeans. Ignoring the city's permit to march only on the sidewalks that lined Fifth Avenue, Friedan took the hands of the suffragist and the radical and then told marchers within earshot to take hands and stretch across the whole street. Following her lead, all protesters joined hands and marched in great swinging long lines from sidewalk to sidewalk. People leaned out of office windows and waved and the marchers shouted back, "Join us!" Protesters brandished banners and placards: "Don't Cook Dinner! Starve a Rat Today!" "Housewives Are Unpaid Slave Laborers!" "Eve Was Framed!"

As planned, the march ended at Bryant Park, behind the New York Public Library at 42nd Street. A speaker's platform had been set up so leaders of the Strike for Equality could use the event as their bully pulpit for continued action. Though others shared the platform, Friedan received the loudest cheers and longest applause. Shouting into the microphone, pumping her firsts in the air, she began:

> After tonight, the politics of this nation will never be the same. By our numbers here tonight, by women who marched curb-to-curb down Fifth Avenue—women who had never marched before in their own cause with veterans of the first battle of the vote . . . young high school students, black women, white women, housewives with women who work in factories and offices, women whose husbands are rich and who discovered that all women are poor—we learned. We learned what none of us had dared to hope—the power of our solidarity, the power of our sisterhood.

In these opening words, Friedan affirmed that she had accomplished what she set out to do: Upset by the fragmentation of the women's movement, she wanted to find some dramatic action that would bring together the warring factions so they, collectively, could realize the empowerment of solidarity. And Friedan wanted this dramatic action to create a nationwide awareness of the moral force and dignity of the women's movement. It is these two achievements that caused Friedan to say later that August 26, 1970, was "one of the happiest days of my life . . . if not *the* happiest." She also knew that her efforts had won significant battles in the unfinished revolution for women, and she anticipated continued victories.

With Betty Friedan at the helm, the National Organization for Women had become a mainstream organization that grew swiftly and was extremely effective. In 1966, NOW had 300 members, most of whom were middle class and centrist in their political views. By 1975, NOW's membership had swelled to 500,000 members whose political views represented the full spectrum of race, gender, class, and sexual orientation. In 1968, NOW forwarded the Bill of Rights for Women as its agenda. By 1975, most demands in that agenda had been met through laws, legislation, and public policies. Understanding the power of mass media, Friedan used sit-ins, marches, protests, and, most especially, the Strike for Equality to effectively broadcast that women would no longer tolerate being treated as second-class citizens. Finally, Friedan had a finely tuned sense of timing: She understood that in the 1960s there was an overarching climate of social reform, and she made sure that NOW and its revolutionary agenda was part of its ecology and weather systems.

Betty Friedan's sheer force of commitment and personality made the early years of NOW successful. Marilyn French suggests that in the late 1960s, Friedan was "catapulted into international prominence" and soon became for many "the symbol of the women's movement." She "worked tirelessly," day and night. She lobbied, organized, and raised funds, and, like a magnet, she drew women from across the country to political activism. Although often a guest at the White House, Friedan also "visited women in labor unions and worked closely with women of color and tried to enlist them in the organization. Her energy seemed limitless; faith and joy buoyed her." Admittedly, achieving success was not easy. After establishing NOW, "Friedan and other leaders," notes French, "had to struggle daily to enable NOW to survive and grow, to be heard over the ridicule of the external world, including the media, and to pierce the silence of women's fear." As Friedan learned, it was almost impossible to unite all women on all issues. Consequently, the fact that Friedan created and sustained a mainstream organization in the women's movement stands as an extraordinary achievement.

Looking back on those early years in 1998, Betty Friedan struggled for her "personal truth" about what the second-wave feminist movement had meant to her and for women. She made these thoughts public in the introduction of a new edition of her book, *It Changed My Life: Writings on the Women's Movement.* From her own questioning, Friedan came to understand that the ideology of the unfinished revolution for women was not necessarily shaped by NOW's Bill of Rights for Women. Rather, this revolution had been shaped by the personal, concrete realities of women's daily lives. As women began to realize the small and large ways how they were oppressed in their daily lives, they made these grievances public and demanded political solutions. Indeed, the personal *is* political.

More significantly, Betty Friedan recalled the "marvelous outpouring of political passion" in herself and others. She used political passion as it had been defined in the ancient Greek city-states. In antiquity, political passion was expected only of "free men, not of slaves or women." As part of the male domain, this political passion also served as "the highest aspect of the human condition: to use one's life to move life forward whether as an artist, a philosopher, or an actor in public life." Then Friedan responds to the Greek's patriarchal mindset: "It was a miracle when women, who were never expected to enter the public sphere at all, did experience that political passion as they sought power to change the possibilities of their own lives."

Implied, but unspoken, this political passion, once unleashed, would continue to move the lives of women as they marched forward to complete their unfinished revolution.

Transcending Polarities

On every side, the women's movement seemed to be leading to impossible confrontations with power—insoluble economic, psychological, sexual, and even theological dilemmas. And yet our new strength and hopes as women also imply value changes in the way we, and men, will love and work and live, earn and buy. . . . It is possible to transcend the polarities? Equality—and the larger values revolution of human liberation—can't be lived unless we do.

Betty Friedan, *It Changed My Life,* 1976

By organizing and leading the Women's March for Equality, Betty Friedan achieved one of her greatest successes as a leader in the second-wave feminist movement. She knew that the march symbolized a significant step forward in completing the unfinished revolution for women while, at the same time, she was aware that this revolution was far from over. Understanding this, Friedan believed she would be significant to its completion. However, she soon discovered that rather than serving as the centrifugal force that energized the women's movement, she had been demoted. No longer the president of NOW, she was pushed aside to an honorary position that merely kept her name on the group's stationery. To younger, more radical, feminists, she was considered as self-serving, an albatross, an elitist, a hypocrite, a liability, and, for some, irrelevant.

Now abandoned, Friedan felt lost. As a leader in the second-wave feminist movement, she had been marginalized, and as a middle-age woman, she was divorced and less essential to her three adolescent children. Cast adrift, Friedan, always resourceful, had to find new moorings to anchor her personal and public lives.

Soon after her divorce, Betty Friedan discovered the Esalen Institute, located at Big Sur, the volcanic coastline in central California. Founded in 1962, the institute focused on the exploration of human potential, much like other counterculture movements that had emerged in the 1960s. At Esalen, encounter groups, sensitivity training, and psychodrama served as upscale consciousness-raising. The infusion of the new psychology of esoteric Eastern philosophies replaced, for Friedan, the dogmatic principles of Marxism and feminist ideologies of sexism and patriarchy. In the summer of 1969, she spent a month at Esalen partaking in group therapy, lying in the natural hot mineral baths that overlooked the Pacific, and participating in a training workshop for therapists. In the 1970s, she often returned to the Esalen Institute because its ambiance and therapies helped her resolve personal issues, holdovers from the past, as well as cope with challenges that she now confronted.

Among these challenges, Friedan had to redefine her relationship with her three children, who were leaving home to begin their journeys as independent adults. Danny, her firstborn, had earned, at age 16, a substantial scholarship at Princeton University in 1964. Overwhelmed by the adult world of his classmates, he left after the first year. He later returned to Princeton, graduated with honors in 1970, and completed graduate work in physics at the University of California, Berkeley in 1980. In 1987, Danny received a five-year fellowship from the MacArthur Foundation, an honor known as the "genius award." In 1970, Jonathan, Friedan's second child, enrolled in Columbia University, located in New York City, and demonstrated his independence by moving to campus. Like his brother, Jonathan dropped out of college after a year, moved to the West Coast, where he decided to work as a salmon fisherman in the San Juan Islands, off the coast of Washington state. After five years at sea, he returned to Columbia and graduated with a degree in engineering. In 1970, Emily, Friedan's youngest child, was a budding teenager of 14. To be closer to her daughter, Friedan had Emily come with her on speaking tours in Brazil (1971) and Italy (1972). When deciding on a college in 1973, Emily chose Radcliffe over Smith College, her mother's alma mater. She completed her studies at Harvard Medical School, specializing in pediatric medicine.

Immeasurably proud of her children's achievements, and more importantly, their independent spirits, Friedan also felt a great void in their absence. To fill this empty space, she decided to reintroduce into her life an "extended family." Recalling that the "happiest years of her life" had been when she and Carl had a close-knit group of friends while living in Parkway Village in the 1950s, Friedan wanted to recapture that sense of commitment. Beginning in the summer of 1970, she recruited friends to join her in renting an old mansion in the Hamptons, a string of towns, villages and hamlets located on eastern Long Island. Her new "chosen family," which she named "The Commune," became the necessary support system that she needed. By all accounts, the summer days and evenings were filled with pastimes like charades, intellectual debates, and shared responsibilities of cleaning and cooking. Although some members of Friedan's chosen family changed, The Commune rented mansions in the Hamptons for four consecutive summers.

Most reassuring in her search for new moorings, Betty Friedan had fallen in love. In a workshop on alternative family lifestyles in 1970, she met David Manning White, a writer and academic. He was handsome with his straight silvery white hair and charming with his courtly southern manners. "I'm not going to say sparks flew or the earth moved when we met," Friedan writes in *Life So Far*. But "there was immediate, mutual chemistry" that evolved into a "wonderful, passionate relationship" that lasted 10 years. Two barriers stood in their way for a long-term, fully satisfying relationship: White lived in Boston whereas Friedan lived in New York, and neither wanted to relocate. The more insurmountable barrier was that White would not divorce his wife because she was wealthy and he was devoted to their five children. Apparently, Betty had few problems with White's constraints; neither did his wife, Catherine, who knew about the affair. Although she dated other men, White was the most important man in Friedan's life in the 1970s. Friedan took him on glamorous trips, where she, as the honored guest, was treated like royalty. When Friedan received two reserved seats for Jimmy Carter's inauguration ceremony in 1977, she and White watched as the new president took the oath of office. In the early 1980s, Friedan and White ended their affair, but that did not end their love. When White died in 1993, Friedan called Catherine. Upset, she told White's widow that she loved David very much. Catherine affirmed that her husband had also loved Friedan, and it was unfortunate that the three of them could not have found a way that they could have all lived together.

While seeking new moorings in her personal life, Betty Friedan also looked for new opportunities to anchor her public life, a challenge far more difficult and conflicted. Although still a member of NOW's Executive Board, she no longer had significant influence in shaping policy. In part, her loss reflected changes in the women's movement. By 1970, feminists in NOW and other mainstream organizations and the radical and lesbian feminists in the women's liberation movement realized that it was time to stop bickering and begin pooling their resources. Otherwise neither the liberal nor the radical wing of the second-wave feminist movement would be successful. What NOW activists offered, notes historian Ruth Rosen, was a national presence, leadership, and organizing skills that made them effective lobbyists, organizers, and strategists. Feminists in the women's liberation groups provided a critique of patriarchal culture, visions of nontraditional lifestyles, the empowerment of consciousness-raising, and the articulation of hidden injuries of sex such as date and spousal rape. As equal contributors, lesbian feminists infused into the women's movement new ideas and theories that helped feminists— and later scholars—to consider the social and cultural construction of gender, as well as the biological nature of sex.

Over the long term, this collaboration made the second-wave feminist movement a stronger and more diverse movement. More immediate, the leadership of NOW shifted its political stance from the mainstream liberalism of Friedan to sexual politics—the demand to dismantle male dominance as a cultural and political reality in American society. The first indicator of this shift was when members of NOW voted to incorporate lesbian rights as part of its statement of purpose in 1971 (see Chapter 7).

Friedan strongly disagreed with this shift in priorities, because she believed it cast NOW as an anti-male organization. However, since she had lost power to shape policies in NOW, she decided to use her political clout to lobby for a woman's right to a legal abortion.

Betty Friedan demonstrated her commitment to reproductive rights when she joined Larry Lader of Planned Parenthood in establishing the National Association for the Repeal of Abortion Laws (NARAL) in 1969. The purpose of NARAL was to pressure elected officials to change abortion laws. Prior to the Supreme Court ruling on *Roe v. Wade* (1973), abortion laws resided in the states. Until the early 1960s, state abortion laws prohibited abortion except for preservation of the mother's life, required medical certification of a life-threatening situation, and the approval of a board of doctors. In 1962, the American Law Institute recommended that states expand their criteria to approve abortions in cases of rape, incest, and evidence of potential fetal deformity, and the American Medical Association (AMA) endorsed these recommendations in 1967.

As part of this greater dialogue about restrictive abortion laws, Friedan, as president and past president of NOW and as cofounder of NARAL, used her power to organize women and men to demand that states repeal current restrictive laws on abortion, replacing these with a law that gave women the legal right to an abortion. Consistently, Friedan took the position that it was a woman's right and decision to abort, not that of the AMA, elected officials in state government, and boards of doctors in communities and cities—all male-dominated bastions of power. By 1970, three states, including New York and California, repealed abortion laws, and by 1972, another 13 states and the District of Columbia had liberalized their abortion laws.

Friedan argued the free-choice platform in speeches, articles, marches, protests, and by lobbying politicians in state legislatures.

But it was at the initial meeting of NARAL in 1969 that she was especially precise and eloquent. She began by making clear that "the right of a woman to control her reproductive process must be established as a basic, inalienable, civil right, not to be endured or abridged by the state—*just as the right of individual and religious conscience is considered an inalienable private right in both the American tradition and in the American Constitution*" (emphasis added). Next, she connected a woman's civil right to an abortion with a personal need to define her identity. Friedan observed that in "a very personal and private way" a woman faced with a decision of ending an unwanted pregnancy had to confront her identity in terms of her sexuality. By making the choice about her pregnancy, no matter the decision, a woman would learn she was not a passive victim; no longer was she merely a sex object who was vulnerable "to the seductions, the waste, the worshipping of false gods in our affluent society." The personal is political, and thereafter, a woman had the potential to live with "full self-determination and full dignity."

The actions of NARAL were instrumental in gaining broader public support for legal abortion. This support became legally tested in the Supreme Court in 1973, when the court justices voted 7 to 2 in favor of *Roe v. Wade*. The Court ruled that state laws that restricted a woman's right to obtain a legal abortion violated the "right to privacy" clause of the Fourteenth Amendment. Therefore, women had the right to legal abortions on demand.

Friedan went to the Supreme Court on January 23, 1973, the day that the court read its decision. She later wrote that on that day in January, she had witnessed a historical moment for women: With *Roe v. Wade*, the nation's highest court finally had interpreted the Constitution "to acknowledge the personhood of women—stating that our right to sexual privacy and the control of our own bodies in the matter of childbearing and abortion was more basic than many of the rights spelled out in the Bill of Rights, as it was written of, by and for men." *Roe v. Wade* immediately affected the lives of millions of women. Maternal deaths from illegal abortions dropped by 600 percent. More significantly, that 900,000 women had safe legal abortions in 1974 proved that abortion had become an option for all women, rather than only those who had money and connections.

Simultaneous to her advocacy for legal abortion, Betty Friedan was a cofounder of the National Women's Political Caucus (NWPC) in 1971. As president of NOW, she had realized that women, who represented 53 percent of the population, had tremendous political clout, and this power was an untapped resource. When she organized the Strike for Equality in 1970, Friedan gained a greater measure of this potential power. She also concluded that NOW was not the right organization to unite women on political issues, a belief likely grounded in the fact that she was no longer its president. Therefore, Friedan decided that women needed a new organization devoted to awakening, organizing, and asserting women's considerable political power.

That Friedan realized the need for an organization devoted to increasing women's political power demonstrates that she had her hand on the pulse of women's sentiments. But hers was not the only hand. Other activists were also aware of the untapped political power of women, and they, too, wanted to establish and lead such an organization. And these activists were not the compliant bureaucrats that Friedan had encountered when founding NOW. Rather, they were Bella Abzug, the aggressive, flamboyant U.S. congresswoman from New York; Shirley Chisholm, the first African American women elected to the U.S. Congress; and Gloria Steinem, protégé and ally of Abzug whose good looks and precise statements caused the media to consider her as spokesperson for the second-wave feminist movement.

There are conflicting stories about whether Friedan or Abzug began NWPC. Friedan claims it was her idea, Abzug claims she and Friedan came up with the idea simultaneously, and Steinem claims that it grew out of a spontaneous idea by both Abzug and Friedan. What became immediately clear, however, was that Friedan's vision for NWPC differed from Abzug's, and Abzug, as a politico, wielded greater power. Friedan envisioned that NWPC would be structured the same as NOW with a national leadership team and local chapters. She also believed the caucus should encourage and support women of both political parties to run for office, lobby for the demands delineated in NOW's Bill of Rights for Women, and give local chapters the autonomy to identify and work for issues most relevant to them. Abzug agreed with Friedan about the organization's structure but strongly disagreed with her approach. Instead Abzug wanted NWPC to support only women running for political office who would work for the issues identified by the national leadership, and these issues in the 1970s demanded progressive social change put forward by women of color and by radical and lesbian feminists. Betty Friedan wanted an organization that made midwestern Republican women welcome; Bella Abzug wanted an organization that built a coalition that centered on young, poor, minority, and radical women.

In this gambit to gain control of NWPC, Friedan lost because Abzug was better at playing hardball politics. More relevant, she lost because Abzug and other activists did not want Friedan to use the organization to bulldoze her mainstream, anti-lesbian, and anti-sexual politics agenda forward. Although everyone agreed on the issues of reproductive rights and the ERA, Abzug and her allies, like the national leadership of NOW, believed the essential issues for women in the early 1970s were welfare rights, race and sex discrimination for women of color, gay rights, rape and spousal abuse, and sexual harassment.

That Abzug and her supporters had taken a more accurate measure of the pulse of the sentiments of feminists was demonstrated at the first meeting of the NWPC held at the Statler Hilton Hotel in Washington, D.C., on July 10 and 11, 1971. Several of the founders and many of the 300 political women who attended that meeting were Hispanic, Native American, and African American women who represented their minority constituencies. Among these were Fannie Lou Hamer, a leader in the Mississippi Freedom Democrats; Lupe Anguiano, Mexican American civil rights activist; and Shirley Chisholm, Democratic congresswoman from New York. Friedan, as one of the founders, opened the meeting. In her remarks, she sought common ground by saying, "What unites women as a majority is the refusal to be manipulated any longer. What unites women across the lines of race, class, generation and man-made party politics is the demand for participation ourselves: our own voice in the big decisions affecting our lives."

No doubt, Friedan felt validated when selected to open the first meeting of the NWPC. But she anticipated greater rewards: At this meeting, she wanted to be elected to the National Steering Committee and to be selected as its spokesperson to the media. She was not elected to the Steering Committee, and committee members selected Steinem to be the organization's official spokesperson. Despite her disappointment, Friedan traveled to several states in 1971 to help organize local chapters. But when she failed to be elected to the National Steering Committee at NWPC's national meeting in 1973, Friedan decided to find other venues to assert her influence. One such option had already come her way.

In 1970, Shana Alexander, editor at *McCall's* magazine, recruited Friedan, who was a friend, to write a column. This column, "Betty Friedan's Notebook," met Friedan's desire to keep her name and agenda for women's rights visible to a considerable number of women. Her primary objective was to reassure readers that the real focus of the second-wave feminist movement was to advocate policies and laws that addressed the needs of women who were wives and mothers. With these objectives in mind, Friedan wrote about a full range of experiences that "women's lib," in her view, either ignored or dismissed as "not relevant" to feminism. In many columns, the author of *The Feminine Mystique* talked about clothes, food, home decor, entertaining, hairdos, children, and happiness with men.

But the columns most remembered were the ones in which Friedan attacked feminists who did not share her mainstream ideas. She used one column, "Everything I Know Has Come from My Own Experience," to argue that the "radical fringe" is destroying the women's movement. In this narrative, she labels radical feminists as "pseudo radicals." She attacks their tactic of consciousness-raising, which she calls "navel-gazing rap sessions," and reduces the pseudo radicals' advocacy of sexual politics to a diatribe on the "meanness of male chauvinist pigs, the comparisons of orgasm, [and] talk about getting rid of love, sex, children, and men." In September 1972, she returned to this theme in "Female Chauvinism Is Dangerous." Readers of that column learn that Bella Abzug and Gloria Steinem are "female chauvinist boors," who are "corrupting our movement for equality and inviting a backlash that endangers the very real gains we have won these past few years." To counter these female chauvinists, Friedan offers readers her definition of feminism, one that recognized that because "women are people, in the fullest sense of the word," they are, therefore, entitled to "all the privileges, opportunities, and responsibilities that are their human and American right."

Friedan expanded her audience and escalated her attacks when she wrote an article for the *New York Times Magazine* in 1973. Entitled "Up from the Kitchen Floor," Friedan tells readers that women who preached "man-hating sex/class warfare" are threatening to take control of NOW. If this happens, these "man-haters" would drive out all women who wanted a husband and children. Those intent on "disrupting" the women's movement, she continues, are "continually trying to push lesbianism or hatred of men." But their motives are not sincere. Rather, Friedan suggests, these disrupters are, in fact, encouraged and trained by the Federal Bureau of Investigation (FBI) and the Central Intelligence Agency (CIA), and their objective is to discredit the women's movement.

Such allegations, though exaggerated, had some basis in fact. Historian Ruth Rosen discovered that female agents were employed by the FBI to infiltrate and monitor the activities of local groups of feminist activists in the 1970s. Their objective, however, was not to discredit the second-wave feminist movement but to gain access to feminist activists who were also part of the radical left's antiwar movement or who were espousing Marxist and communist ideologies. With the benefit of hindsight and scholarship, historians agree that any infiltration by the FBI or the CIA did not damage the credibility of the women's movement nearly as much as those within the movement who continuously and viciously attacked each other. Betty Friedan was not alone in making these attacks, but she most certainly was among the loudest and most noticed.

Moreover, Friedan's ongoing public diatribes put her in conflict with the leadership of NOW. Those members who had successfully campaigned to get lesbian rights added to NOW's agenda in 1971 took control of the organization's national leadership by 1974.

Calling themselves the Majority Caucus, these leaders had a new slogan, "Out of the Mainstream into the Revolution," and identified its agenda as a revolution against male oppressors. Alarmed by these events, Friedan publicly denounced the leadership and had secret meetings with her mainstream supporters where they conspired on how to take control of NOW. Although they never followed through, Friedan's actions contributed to NOW evolving into an organization wracked by divisiveness and internal power struggles, as well as increasing her reputation as a pariah.

Added to increased rejection in the women's movement, Betty Friedan had failed to meet her contract obligation with Random House for a second book. She had signed a book contract with the publishing house in 1964, promised the book in three years, and spent the entire $30,000 advance. By the early 1970s, the editors had lost their patience. Books on the second wave of feminism had become a new hot topic for publishers and readers. Random House wanted its market share and hoped that a book by the author of *The Feminine Mystique* would help secure it.

The underlying problem that Friedan faced was that her original concept—to evaluate the new life patterns of women who had moved beyond the feminine mystique—was no longer relevant. Given this, she decided to reconfigure the book's contents as a contemporary history about the way that the second-wave feminist movement had changed her life as well as the lives of numerous other women. By so doing, Friedan could anchor the book in the safe harbor of her own journey in the women's movement. Editors at Random House liked the new proposal and renegotiated the contract by providing an additional advance and a due date of February 4, 1975, which, by happenstance, was Friedan's 54th birthday. Friedan met her deadline, and Random House published Friedan's second book, *It Changed My Life: Writings on the Women's Movement* in 1976; it then sold the paperback reprint rights to Dell for $100,000.

Friedan's second book was not a success. The hardcover version had limited sales, and the paperback version fell far short of the record sales of *The Feminine Mystique*. Comments by reviewers were lukewarm. The biggest problem was that in the process of telling "her story," Friedan continued to attack those who opposed her and failed to explore fairly the complexity of the issues facing feminists. Her section on the establishment of the NWPC, for example, is highly self-serving, polemical, and inaccurate. In response to Friedan's account, 26 members of the NWPC sent a letter to Random House stating, quite accurately, that Friedan's account was marred by "factual errors, self-serving fiction, racist assumptions, and character assassinations."

With the distance of time, *It Changed My Life* has gained credibility as an account of the second wave of feminism. It provides a running history of the women's movement from the late 1940s through the early 1970s from the vantage point of Betty Friedan, who defined much of what that movement was all about. Thus, in retrospect, the strong reaction in the 1970s against her running history of the movement serves as another example that Friedan had been banished from the movement by feminist activists.

While struggling to finish her second book, Betty Friedan looked for new venues to promote her vision for women's full equality. Starting in 1973, she was offered, and accepted, a series of visiting professorships. Among the first was a position to teach one day each week at Temple University in Philadelphia. Asked specifically to integrate her experiences as a feminist activist into her courses, Friedan used her insights and perspectives in an undergraduate course, "Contemporary Social Issues," and a graduate seminar, "The Sex Role Revolution, Stage II." She continued to teach this graduate course at Yale University (New Haven, Connecticut) in 1974 and at Queens College (Brooklyn, New York) in 1975. The content and evolution of "Sex Role Revolution, Stage II" provided Friedan a sounding board to test her ideas about the direction of the women's movement and to help her formulate ideas that were to become the foundation for her next book, *The Second Stage* (1981).

Friedan also accepted a one-semester position as visiting professor at the New School of Social Research in New York City where she had first taught writing classes in the 1950s. In 1970, Friedan's course, "Women in the City," asked students to confront the socioeconomic problems as women living in the greater New York City area. Through dialogues and discussions among the nearly one hundred women who registered for the class, Friedan learned about the financial problems faced by women who were married or divorced; employed, job hunting, or on welfare—white, black, or brown. These women revealed that their essential problem was less the need to earn more money than it was to have greater control over their finances. Their expressed needs prompted Friedan to find a way to start a bank for women. By 1975, her efforts led to The First Women's Bank and Trust Company, located in New York City, and, as a founder, she served as one of its first directors. As one who advocated a woman's right to full equality, Friedan must have been proud that the First Women's Bank marked the fourth organization that she had been instrumental in establishing in less than a decade. Its predecessors were NOW (1966), NARAL (1969), and the NWPC (1971).

Betty Friedan also used her reputation to foster a greater awareness of women's rights in foreign countries. By combining the invitations to lecture and her assignments from *McCall's* and other publications, she traveled to the Middle East, Europe, and Latin America in the 1970s. In 1973, Friedan had three encounters that she found most noteworthy. The first was when Friedan went to Israel to speak at a meeting of an international organization of women writers and journalists, who were motivated and inspired by her ideas. She anticipated a meeting with Golda Meir, the first, and only, female prime minister of Israel. Instead, Friedan discovered that Meir had no time to meet with her, even though she was in Israel for two weeks. She was also dismayed when the prime minister made clear in public speeches that she did not favor a replication of a women's movement for equality for the State of Israel. The disconnect between Meir's strong leadership skills and her seemingly antifeminist attitudes puzzled, as well as disappointed, Friedan.

Later that year, Friedan requested, and was granted, a private audience with Pope Paul VI. This surprised her because her views on birth control, abortion, and women's full equality opposed proclamations made by the Catholic Church. Vatican protocol called for an exchange of gifts. When they met, Paul VI spoke first and then gave Friedan his gift, a small jewel box. Speaking in English, the pope said, "We want to express our gratitude and appreciation for all you have done for the women of the world." Friedan then gave Pope Paul VI her gift—a chain with the gold-plated symbol of women's equality. "This is a symbol of the women's movement—the sign of the female, in biology, crossed by the sign of absolute equality," Friedan said. "As Your Holiness can see, when women are completely equal to men, it becomes a different kind of cross." Pope Paul VI graciously accepted her gift but not her point of view. What followed was a brief but pointed conversation, in which the two leaders expressed to one another their personal and political points of view about the personhood of women. Neither convinced the other, but each gained a greater measure and respect for the personhood of the other.

From Rome, Friedan went to Paris because she finally had succeeded in getting an interview with Simone de Beauvoir, author of *The Second Sex* (1949). Friedan anticipated as a

Betty Friedan gives the women's medal to Pope Paul VI, 1973.
© The Schlesinger Library, Radcliffe Institute, Harvard University.

consequence of this meeting that de Beauvoir would agree to issue a joint statement with her about the women's movement. Their statement, which would have been published in *McCall's* magazine, would ask feminists to refocus their efforts away from the anti-man, anti-motherhood, anti-marriage of sexual politics because these attitudes did not speak to the attitudes of most women in American and French societies. Perhaps Friedan was too blinded by her own feminist ideology or she had mis-read de Beauvoir's *The Second Sex*. Nonetheless, their conversa-tion made clear that she and de Beauvoir disagreed on virtually everything. And instead of the joint statement, Friedan's article for *McCall's* is a dialogue between two feminists, neither of whom was willing to listen to the other.

The more significant insight that Friedan gained from her trav-els and contacts was the realization that the momentum of the second-wave feminist movement was, in her view, "sweeping the globe with America leading the charge." By 1973, Betty Friedan joined forces with Patricia Burnett, who had founded the Michigan chapter of NOW and had become president of NOW International. Working as a team, they helped organize 25 chap-ters of NOW in 21 countries and gained NGO (Non-Government Organization) status for NOW. Based on her travels, Friedan believed that women in these affiliate chapters should meet. Needing funds, she appealed to her friend Stewart Mott, a philan-thropist dedicated to supporting efforts that promote a just, equi-table, and sustainable society. Then she persuaded the woman president of Lesley College, located in Cambridge, Massachusetts, to provide meeting rooms. Friedan and Burnett's efforts led to the International Feminist Planning Conference, which was sponsored by NOW and convened for three days in December 1973. More than 300 women from 27 countries attended this meeting, includ-ing women from Arab countries, Israel, and the Soviet Union.

Although gratified by this meeting, Friedan and Burnett real-ized this group included only wealthy women. To make women's rights a centerpiece of human rights required the support of a high-profile international organization. Therefore, they arranged to meet with Kurt Waldheim, the secretary-general of the United Nations (UN). In this meeting, they suggested that the UN could advance human rights on an international scale by promoting and financially supporting an international conference where women from UN member nations could meet to explore their needs and constraints within their own countries. Waldheim agreed.

Waldheim had the UN designate 1975 as International Women's Year (IWY), and the UN organized and sponsored an international conference in Mexico City. The success of that meeting caused the UN to expand its support to the Decade for Women (1976–1985) and followed the Mexico City conference with ones in Stockholm (1980) and Nairobi (1985). (The UN sponsored an additional meeting in Beijing in 1995.) During the Decade for Women, the UN focused on various activities that connected the needs of women with the demand for social justice and equity. Friedan attended all four international conferences but was disappointed by the outcomes. Each conference, in its own way, served as a battleground for international politics. In the UN conferences for women, attendees were sincere in their calls for human rights and plans for action to advance equality of women, but the male-dominated political power structures of their nation-states used these meetings as venues for Cold War politics.

In the midst of finding new venues to promote her feminist ideas, Betty Friedan must have felt a great sense of achievement. Most items that she had identified as demands in NOW's Bill of Rights for Women (1968) had or were poised to become realities. Between 1971 and 1974, Congress enacted unprecedented equity laws: an end to sex discrimination in hiring, income tax deductions for child care if both spouses worked, the end of creditors' practice of denying loans and credit on the basis of sex and marital status, extension of the 1963 Equal Pay Act by inclusion of an education amendment, and an additional equity act that supported training and counseling programs for women.

Most especially, Friedan felt validated that a woman's right for a legal abortion, one of her two gut issues listed in the Bill of Rights for Women, had been sanctioned by the Supreme Court's ruling on *Roe v. Wade*. And she anticipated that her other gut issue, the Equal Rights Amendment (ERA), would be added to the U.S. Constitution.

Written by Alice Paul in 1921, the original text of the ERA states that "men and women shall have equal rights throughout the United States and every place subject to its jurisdiction." This meant that women would be freed from legal sex discrimination. Paul's amendment was introduced to the U.S. Congress in 1923, but it stayed buried in congressional committees until 1970. Largely through the efforts of Friedan, as president of NOW, the Senate Subcommittee on Constitutional Amendments began hearings on this amendment in 1970, and it moved from the House Judiciary Committee to consideration by the House of Representatives. By 1972, both the House of Representatives and the Senate had approved the ERA by overwhelming majorities, 354 to 23 in the House and 84 to 8 in the Senate. Following congressional approval, the ERA gained endorsements from the National Education Association, the United Auto Workers, the League of Women Voters, and the America Federation of Labor and Congress of Industrial Workers (AFL-CIO).

Gaining congressional support and major endorsements for the ERA was a significant victory for NOW. Passionate about this issue, Friedan consistently argued that the ERA, unlike laws, executive orders, and even court rulings, could not be easily undone—it would assure that "men and women shall have equal rights throughout the United States and every place subject to its jurisdiction," whether conservatives or liberals controlled the Congress.

As a proposed amendment to the U.S. Constitution, the ERA had to be ratified by three-fourths of the states (38 states) by a two-thirds majority vote in the state legislatures, and Congress granted seven years (1972–1979) for this process. With Hawaii taking the lead, 30 states ratified the amendment by 1973, and ratification in eight more states seemed certain. Despite early success, the ERA was still three states short of ratification by 1977, and battles in these states would be uphill. Concerned, NOW successfully pressured Congress to extend the ratification deadline until 1982.

The ERA had significant opposition. Opposition, in part, originated with the election of Richard Nixon as president in 1968. His election signaled a shift in the political temperament of the nation from the political liberalism that called for aggressive social reform to a conservative resurgence that replaced the sexual revolution with family values. Although Nixon publicly supported the ERA, he privately told his advisers that he hoped the good sense and ultimate wisdom of Congress would keep "this ridiculous proposal from being enacted." In addition, Nixon demonstrated his opposition to women breaking away from their traditional gender roles when he vetoed the Comprehensive Child Development Bill in 1972. This legislation would have provided a nationwide network of child-care centers funded by the federal government. Nixon stated that he vetoed the bill because it called for a "communal approach to child rearing" and it would weaken the family.

The more significant and pervasive opposition to the ERA came from Phyllis Schlafly, whose antifeminist views harped on the potential negative consequences for women and their families if the amendment were ratified. Born in St. Louis, Missouri, three years later than Friedan, Schlafly shaped her political and antifeminist perspectives from her politically and socially conservative parents, midwestern roots, and Catholic faith and education. She married a lawyer in the late 1940s, had six children, and lived an upper-middle-class lifestyle that enabled her to combine her role as homemaker and her interest as a political activist in the Republican Party. She became known for her best-selling 1964 book *A Choice, Not an Echo,* which argued for supporting Barry Goldwater, a conservative senator from Arizona, in his bid for the presidency in 1964. The title of her book became Goldwater's campaign slogan, and she campaigned tirelessly for his election.

In the late 1960s and early 1970s, Schlafly, when asked, consistently stated that she was "indifferent" to feminism. Her indifference, however, took a sharp turn to the political right in 1972. That year, Schlafly founded and led the Eagle Forum as one of the first right-to-life organizations. Still active today, the organization's mission statement is to "enable conservative and pro-family men and women to participate in the process of self-government and public-policy making so that America will continue to be a land of individual liberty, respect for family integrity, public and private virtue, and private enterprise." To alert members of the

Eagle Forum about important issues, she published the "Phyllis Schlafly Report." It was in this newsletter that she first attacked the ERA in 1972. Soon thereafter, she organized the "Stop the ERA" movement, complete with banners and buttons that put STOP ERA on an image of the STOP sign used to regulate traffic. She defined the word STOP as "*Stop Taking Our Privileges.*"

In her newsletter and speeches, Schlafly pointed out that a "sexless society" would upset the delicate balance of specific roles and responsibilities taken by a wife and husband in marriage. It was these specific roles, Schlafly argued, that assured women their special privileges. She also impressed on her converts that lesbianism and the ERA were connected. She preached that the "ERA would put 'gay rights' into the U.S. Constitution because the *word* in the amendment is '*sex*,' not '*women*'" (emphasis added). And to heighten the fear factor, she asserted that "eminent authorities have stated that ERA would legalize the granting of marriage licenses to same-sex couples and generally implement the gay and lesbian agenda."

Finally, and skillfully, Schlafly identified the enemy: NOW. Rhetorically, she would ask, 'Why is NOW pressuring for the ERA?' Then she answered: NOW had a hidden agenda: It supported legislation and court decisions that assured the civil rights of lesbians. NOW supported abortion on demand. NOW lobbied for federal legislation that would allow pornography, busing, and black power. Thus, in organizing the STOP ERA movement, Phyllis Schlafly created a grassroots network of women whose social, political, and religious conservatism made them afraid of feminists swept up in the second-wave feminist movement. Once she convinced these countless women of the logic of antifeminism, she led the crusade to defeat the ERA.

More significantly, the feuds within NOW had a greater impact on the ratification process of the ERA. By the mid-1970s, the organization was wracked with debates and conflicts among mainstream members, whose power was at the local and state levels, and radical members, who controlled NOW at the national level. In addition, NOW, buoyed by early victories in the ratification process, failed to make the ERA a priority in the mid-1970s. Instead, it redirected its political clout to lobby for gay rights, federally funded child care, the need to increase antipoverty programs for single mothers, date and spousal rape, sexual harassment, and reproductive freedoms offered by new technologies such as artificial insemination and so-called test tube babies. Such an agenda obviously gave Schlafly more ammunition in her STOP ERA campaign.

Finally, most feminists dismissed Schlafly's antifeminism as "irrelevant." They failed to understand that mainstream and conservative women feared the consequences of feminist agendas, most especially if these agendas promoted lesbianism and a sexual revolution that identified men as the enemy. However, there was one avowed feminist—Betty Friedan—who foresaw the destructive forces of infighting among various factions in the second wave of feminism.

Still powerful, Friedan was unrelenting in her efforts to return NOW to its mainstream roots and to silence radical feminists. Otherwise, she feared the ERA would fail. It was this political reality that caused Friedan to be so strident and vocal about what she called the "radical fringe." Yet under that tough exterior of abusive accusations, Friedan was heartfelt in her desire that women would no longer feel the despair of "the problem that has no name," that they would no longer be considered sex objects, and that they no longer would be second-class citizens who had, at best, limited power to effect change. Friedan wanted, as she had written in 1973, feminists to understand that "the women's movement . . . is a stage in the whole human rights movement" that would bring "another group, a majority this time, into the mainstream of human society. . . . No more, no less."

Not willing to settle for anything less, Betty Friedan continued to hope, longing for an event such as the Women's March for Equality in 1970 that would make feminists, once again, understand that their power resided in the solidarity of their sisterhood.

New Feminist Frontiers

In the religion of my ancestors, men used to pray each day thanking God for not being women. And women prayed simply to submit themselves to the Lord's will. Not anymore. I believe all women all over the world will be able to say, I thank you, Lord, for making me a woman.

Betty Friedan, March for Women's Equality, 1970

Betty Friedan had a knack for making things happen. Often, she consciously seized an advantage and turned it into an organization or event. Establishing NOW is a prime example. At other times, she served as a catalyst, setting into motion a series of actions that led to change. Betty Friedan was the catalyst that led to the National Women's Conference in 1977, a meeting that marks the high point of the second of wave of feminism.

As described in Chapter 8, Friedan and Pat Burnett, president of NOW International, met with Kurt Waldheim, the UN secretary-general in late 1973. In part, their meeting led to the UN declaring 1975 International Women's Year and supporting an international conference in Mexico City, where Friedan was a leading force. At Mexico City, delegates decided that each member country needed to adopt a national plan of action for women. Friedan saw the mandate for a national plan of action as an opportunity to refocus the women's movement in the United

States on the essential issues that would secure women's full equality in American society.

Once she returned from Mexico City, Friedan, as well as other prominent activists in the second-wave feminist movement, wanted to capitalize on this need for a national plan of action by getting financial support from the federal government for a national conference. Bella Abzug, a powerful force in Congress, parlayed the UN mandate into gaining congressional support and securing five million dollars in government funding for the National Women's Conference. This conference was scheduled for November 18 to 21, 1977, and would be held in Houston, Texas. At that conference, delegates would agree on a national plan that promoted "equality between men and women" in the United States, and this plan, presumably, would serve as a model for other nations. Politically astute, Abzug, as presiding officer of the conference, assembled a small group to organize the meeting. Excluded was Friedan, who had, by this time, burned too many bridges. Not completely ignored, however, Friedan attended the conference as a delegate at large, and as it turned out, she made a significant contribution to its success.

The National Women's Conference was the first national women's conference to be sponsored by the federal government, and such sponsorship gave the second-wave feminist movement national recognition. Although not feminist in name or official status, with Abzug at the helm and funds to spend, it was as if feminists had finally come of age because they could employ government organizations, personnel, and funds to further their cause. To affirm their support for the women's movement, Lady Bird Johnson and Betty Ford, two former First Ladies, and Rosalyn Carter, the current First Lady, attended the conference. The national conference brought together a coalition of more than forty organizations, making this conference the single most unified and largest gathering of the women's movement.

Delegates to the conference were selected at assemblies in each of the 50 states, and these delegates were to make recommendations for and vote on the National Plan of Action. At the grassroots level, 2,005 delegates were elected at special community meetings, and some state delegations included men. Most delegates were feminists, and members of racial and ethnic groups were selected in proportions greater than their percentage in the general population. About 20 percent of the delegates were opposed to feminist ideas, and the majority of them came from politically conservative states where legalized abortion, the ERA, and lesbian rights were unpopular.

In addition to the elected delegates, over 4,000 people, including 100 women from foreign countries and a considerable number from the media, gathered in Houston to observe the conference and, in some cases, to pressure delegates on certain planks in the National Plan of Action. Lesbian activists, for example, came to Houston to lobby for a resolution for lesbian rights in the national plan. More significant, 15,000 members of STOP ERA, led by Phyllis Schlafly, came to Houston. These antifeminists publicly denounced the National Women's Conference and feminists' advocacy for abortion, the ERA, and lesbian rights as "sick," "immoral," "ungodly," "unpatriotic," and "antifamily."

That the federal government had sanctioned and funded the National Women's Conference also made it an event worthy of media coverage. Thus planners of the conference decided to assure maximum coverage by having a 2,600-mile torch relay from Seneca Falls, New York, the location of the first women's conference in 1848, to Houston, Texas, the site for the second women's conference. Poet Maya Angelou wrote a new Declaration of Sentiments to parallel the one passed by the 1848 convention; this declaration accompanied the torch on its journey. The torch was lit at Seneca Falls on September 29 and then carried to Houston, arriving on November 17, the day before the conference began. For the last few miles of the relay, the torch was carried by three young female runners from Houston: a Hispanic, an African American, and a Caucasian. About a mile from the convention center, hundreds of delegates, including Friedan, waited in spattering rain for the torch bearers. Once they arrived, the crowd, led by Abzug, followed the runners to the convention center. Inside the center, the runners and marchers were greeted by the delegates who rose, cheered, and applauded.

At the official opening ceremony the next day, conference organizers presented the torch and Angelou's "Declaration of Sentiments," which had been signed by members of the conference, to Rosalyn Carter, Betty Ford, and Lady Bird Johnson. Next, each First Lady spoke about herself as a woman, not just as the wife of a successful politician. Then Angelou read her heartfelt rendition of a new "Declaration of Sentiments." Calling it "To Form a More Perfect Union," she read in "solemn recognition" that "we recognize that no nation can boast of balance until each member of that nation is equally employed and equally rewarded" and, as women, "we make these promises" to all women in America. Angelou's words must have given Friedan a great sense of satisfaction because they echoed her vision.

Once the conference officially opened, the delegates began to consider and debate proposed resolutions for the National Plan of Action. Each state delegation had come up with a list, and these had been redrafted into 26 resolutions. The final set of resolutions addressed the needs of battered, disabled, minority, rural, poor, young and older women; a woman's right to control her own reproductive life; the need for an Equal Rights Amendment; and the demand to end discrimination based on sexual orientation. The right to an abortion, the ERA, and lesbian rights caused the most acrimonious debate among delegates. Among these three, the one that affirmed lesbian rights was the most divisive and had the greatest potential of derailing support on other proposed resolutions, most especially the ERA. Some 130 feminist-lesbian delegates strenuously argued that a feminist agenda that did not include equal rights regardless of sexual preference was a contradiction in terms, whereas conservative delegates did not want to taint America's national plan of action with gay rights. And delegates on all sides of the debate wondered what Betty Friedan would do or say.

Friedan had an established track record: She opposed inclusion of lesbian rights and a lesbian-feminist agenda in NOW and in all organized efforts of the women's movement. She had been consistent, vicious, and, in some cases, slanderous in her statements. Yet, by 1977, she had one focus—the ERA—which was three states short of ratification. Friedan also knew that she had power: She was still the most important feminist voice of her generation; she had gained international recognition as a feminist; she always attracted large crowds in speaking engagements in the United States; she had just published *It Changed My Life;* and she always attracted the attention of the media. Therefore, what Betty Friedan might or might not say at Houston would matter a great deal.

Friedan feared that a long divisive debate on the lesbian rights resolution might derail the resolution supporting the ERA. She also knew that if she publicly supported the resolution, it would pass quickly. So before the debate on the lesbian rights reached a fever pitch, she decided to speak to the delegates. When Friedan took the microphone, there was an expectant hush in the convention hall. Then she spoke:

> I am considered to be violently opposed to the lesbian issue in the women's movement, and I have been. This issue has been used to divide us and disrupt us and has been seized on by our enemies to try and turn back the whole women's movement to equality, and alienate our support. As a woman of middle age who grew up in Middle America—in Peoria, Illinois—and who has loved men maybe too well, I have my personal hang-ups on this issue. I have made mistakes, we have all made mistakes in our focus on this issue. But now we must transcend our previous differences to devote our full energies to get the Equal Rights Amendment ratified, or we will lose all we have gained. Since . . . we know that the Equal Rights Amendment will do nothing whatsoever for homosexuals, we must support the separate civil rights of our lesbian sisters.

Betty Friedan had apologized for her past actions. And her apology was clearly accepted when most delegates cheered and applauded. As one of the most emotional moments of the conference, her brief statement accomplished what Friedan had set out to do: It stopped a long and acrimonious debate.

After Friedan's statement, the delegates voted. When 80 percent of the delegates passed this resolution, a group of lesbians in the balcony released yellow and blue balloons labeled WE ARE EVERYWHERE. Lesbian activists gathered outside the convention center while delegates voted. Some were dressed in mannish garb and had arrived on motorcycles. Once the votes had been tallied, they joined their supporters inside the convention hall, snake dancing across the floor and cheering, "Thank you, sisters." The television networks recorded the balloons, the cheering, and the snake dancing, and the footage was broadcast around the nation.

That day might well have been a victory for feminists who advocated lesbian rights. But it was even a larger victory for Phyllis Schlafly. Across town, she and members of the STOP ERA movement watched the televised versions of the pro-lesbian celebration at the National Women's Conference. They were pleased that the lesbian rights resolution had passed and even more delighted with the "We Are Everywhere" celebration. Schlafly used this media footage as evidence of the connection between lesbianism and the amendment in her media campaign against the ERA. In 1988, Shelia Tobias, a delegate at the Houston conference, interviewed Schlafly. Tobias asked her when she knew she had won the fight against the ERA. Without flinching, Schlafly replied: It was in Houston, "when the 'libbers' voted for the sexual preference plank, extending the feminist platform to include lesbian rights."

Friedan, like Schlafly, understood that the public display of feminist solidarity with lesbian rights and the specter that WE ARE EVERYWHERE threatened support for the ERA. Most of the 400 delegates (20 percent) who voted against the lesbian rights resolution in Houston represented states that had not yet ratified the ERA. Unless these delegates and their constituencies could be persuaded that this amendment would secure the equal rights for women, including those who chose to be wives and mothers, ratification would fail. As noted in Chapter 8, the ERA was still three states short of ratification in 1977, which had prompted NOW to pressure Congress to extend the ratification deadline to 1982. The ERA had not yet been ratified by any southern state, by Illinois and Missouri, or by Utah, Nevada, and Arizona. ERA advocates were faced with persuading constituents in three of these states by June 1982. As the process unfolded, they targeted states where ratification might be possible.

With this in mind, Betty Friedan decided to focus her campaign for the ERA by gaining support from mainstream women and men. This meant she had to fight for the ERA on the political turf that Phyllis Schlafly had already cultivated. Friedan needed to discredit Schlafly's "Stop Taking Our Privileges" by highlighting that the ERA would secure equal partnership between women and men in both the private and public spheres. As a member of the executive board, she pressured NOW to organize its efforts and funds to lobby for the ERA, and she parlayed her notoriety to speak at state fund-raising events, to lobby politicians in the state legislatures, and to be a visible participant in pro-ERA marches.

Friedan worked especially hard in her home state of Illinois. When she went to Peoria in 1978 for her 40-year high school reunion, she asked the local chapter of NOW to organize a pro-ERA march. Not expecting a large turnout, she was overjoyed when about a thousand people, including some of her Republican friends, gathered for a torchlight parade. "A thousand for Peoria is the equivalent of a million in New York," she later wrote. On Mother's Day 1980, Friedan was one of 100,000 people who marched in Chicago in support of the ERA. Friedan later commented that the turnout for the Chicago march was "astounding in these days of [political] apathy" and "greater than any presidential candidate could summon."

Speaking at rallies, lobbying at state legislatures, and participating in marches were only part of Friedan's efforts to convince mainstream women and men to support the ERA. She committed time and energy to writing pro-ERA articles that were published in *Redbook* magazine, the *New York Times Magazine,* and other mainstream publications. In 1979, Friedan secured a contract from Summit Books to collect these articles and add new material in her third book, *The Second Stage*. This time, Friedan met her publication deadline of 1982. The potential to shift votes in key states for ratification of the ERA motivated her to complete the book quickly.

The Second Stage harkened back to themes that Friedan had already presented in *The Feminine Mystique*, in NOW's Statement

Betty Friedan leads an Equal Rights Amendment march in Washington, D.C., July 9, 1978. © AP Images.

of Purpose and its Women's Bill of Rights, and in all her diatribes against radical and lesbian feminists. She had consistently claimed that the majority of women who sought equality looked for ways to integrate their desires to be wives and mothers with their desire to contribute their talents and ideas to the larger society. Friedan refocused these familiar themes by spotlighting the family as the "new feminist frontier." She had not changed her fundamental assumptions. Rather, by using interviews and data from studies on the family and the economy, she shifted the argument from women's rights to family rights. She noted that according to government statistics, only 11 percent of American households had the "traditional" configuration of a wage-earning father, a full-time homemaking mother, and one or more children. This fact implied that either out of desire or out of economic necessity, younger women would need to choose to have children or to have a profession. If they chose both, then they would have two full-time jobs: one in the workplace and one as a homemaker.

Betty Friedan's point was that the family was at risk. To rectify this situation, women and men, in partnership, must pressure businesses and the government for policies and programs that are "family friendly." Employee benefits should include parental leave, flexible time, on-site child-care facilities, and an assurance that reduced working hours would not threaten job status or promotion. Equally important, state and federal governments must offer tax vouchers or credits to families to compensate for child-care expenses and tax incentives to community organizations to develop quality, yet affordable, child-care facilities for working parents. To make this "new feminist frontier" of family rights a reality, reasoned Friedan, required ratification of the ERA.

By making the family "the new frontier for women's rights," Betty Friedan attacked Phyllis Schlafly's claim that the ERA would destroy the family. But by arguing for the ERA on the cultivated turf of Schlafly's "Stop the ERA" language, Friedan alienated feminists because her argument ignored the reasons why they wanted the ERA ratified: Feminists supported the ERA because it would assure the inalienable rights of all women as a matter of law not of public policy.

Friedan knew the risks but decided to gamble. She took a long shot that she could persuade mainstream and conservative women that the ERA would not threaten their choice to be wives and mothers. By so doing, she played the odds that feminists would understand her strategy. But Friedan gambled and lost. Schlafly had more credibility and loyalty among mainstream women than she did. And feminists considered Friedan a traitor whose concept of the family as "the new feminist frontier" was almost antifeminist.

But this rough-and-tumble arena of feminist politics bothered Friedan far less than the ultimate defeat of the ERA. In June 1982, the deadline for ratification, the ERA was still three states short of ratification. One of these was her home state of Illinois. The defeat of the ERA also marked the end of the second wave of feminism.

Battle weary from the final campaigns for the ERA and now in her 60s, Betty Friedan needed to slow down, rest, and think through how she wanted to spend her last years as a public figure. Much like she had done in the early 1970s, she returned to rethinking her priorities and to enriching relationships with her children and friends. In the midst of battling for an ERA victory, Friedan made a significant step forward. In 1978, she purchased a home in Sag Harbor, one of the communities in the Hamptons. More than a summer getaway, her new home became a refuge and a gathering place for family and friends for over 20 years. Like she had done many times before, Betty decorated with bright print fabrics that made the living areas cheerful and casual. She hung abstract paintings on the living room walls and prominently displayed a sampler that read, "A Woman's Place Is in the World" on the wall near the fireplace.

Another feature was the spacious backyard that sloped down to the Sag Harbor Cove, which became the setting for frequent parties with friends and family. More meaningful, this backyard with its vista was the setting for the marriage of two of her children, Jonathan and Emily. In 1981, Jonathan married Helen Nakdimen, who taught nursery school and eventually became a rabbi. In 1984, Emily, now a medical doctor, married Eli Farhi, also a doctor. To make these weddings complete, Carl Friedan came and participated in the festivities. Daniel, the eldest, married in 1989 but not at the Sag Harbor home. His wife, Ragnheidur Gudmundsdottir (Agga), was a native of Iceland and had two children from a previous marriage. Like Daniel, she, too, is a physicist.

The Sag Harbor home became the "home base" for the Friedan family. Family gatherings were frequent and usually included Carl Friedan. In many ways, Betty's home at Sag Harbor engendered strong ties among her adult children, their spouses, and Carl. By 1993, Friedan was the proud grandmother of eight grandchildren—six biological grandchildren and two step-grandchildren. One can imagine the Friedan clan gathered around the long dining table that seated the entire family as they talked about their lives and ideas. Friends of Friedan who had been part of her life through the painful and tumultuous years of the 1960s and 1970s took notice that their friend had mellowed. Having purchased, decorated, and made her own home as her family's home base helped soften the hard edges of Betty Friedan's public persona.

Perhaps calmer, but not unflagging in her advocacy for women's equality, Friedan understood how the defeat of the ERA had ended the women's movement. Now under siege by the pervasive conservative temperament of national politics, the women's movement encountered barriers and road blocks. The election of Ronald Reagan in 1980, the cultural and political clout of the Moral Majority, and the broad-based support for the right-to-life movement gutted the agenda and ended the influence of feminist activists. Betty Friedan, not one to wave a white flag of defeat, consistently sought new opportunities to effect change in the "largeness, diffuseness, and diversity" of the postfeminist environment.

In finding a place in the postfeminist environment, Friedan decided to expend her energies and influence as a thinker, not as a leader of women's organizations. Thus she continued to seek out and accept appointments as a distinguished scholar at research universities and institutes. In this way, she continued to test her ideas in graduate seminars and public symposiums on ways to advance the personhood of women, to collaborate with scholars and educators, and to gain access to cutting-edge research studies on demographic shifts and social policies. Friedan pursued two interests in the 1980s and 1990s: the "mystique of aging" and the family as the new frontier of feminism. Initially, she focused on the "mystique of aging," a project she had started in the 1970s.

In 1978, Robert Butler invited Betty Friedan to have lunch with him at the Cosmos Club, a prestigious membership club considered to be the social headquarters of the intellectual elite in Washington, D.C. At that time, Butler, a physician interested in gerontology, had won the Pulitzer Prize for *Why Survive? Growing Old in American* (1975) and was the founding director of the National Institute on Aging of the National Institutes of Health (1975–82). In his book and at the institute, Butler expressed concern about how the medical understanding of the aging process had limited its scope only to the physical and mental deterioration associated with aging, such as heart disease and dementia. In the pursuit to develop a "new gerontology," one that promoted active living and longevity, Butler wanted Friedan to investigate why women outlived men. Over lunch, he told her that all the theory and policy on aging was about men, despite the fact that women, who typically lived eight years longer than men, comprised most of the population over age 65. Therefore, women in their golden years were being discriminated against by both the medical community and by public policy.

Friedan was interested: A study of the aging process of women would be another dimension of women's right to equality. Further, Butler's posed questions were the same questions she had pondered in a column for "Betty Friedan's Notebook" in the early 1970s. In that column, Friedan told readers about her own mother, Miriam, who, then in her 70s, had embraced an active lifestyle as a resident in Leisure World, an upscale retirement community in South Orange County, California. When Friedan went to Southern California to attend the annual meeting of NOW in 1972, her mother drove to the convention hotel. Miriam wanted to see her daughter and, more importantly, she wanted to be part of the NOW meeting, an experience she very much enjoyed.

Friedan made significant points in the column about her mother's active and fulfilling lifestyle. Readers learned that Miriam had married twice after the death of Friedan's father and had survived both husbands. Then they discovered that Miriam, at age 70, had started a new career, using her lifelong skills at playing bridge to get licensed as a manager of duplicate bridge tournaments that were held throughout Southern California. Then two years later, she took up horseback riding for exercise, and at age 74, she started another "career" distributing ecologically sound biodegradable detergents, cosmetics, and vitamins. Then Friedan closes her entry in "Betty Friedan's Notebook" with an observation that in spending time with her 74-year-old mother, she suddenly realized, "how many millions of men and women like my mother, still moving toward life in their 70s and 80s, must rebel against being walled up in nursing homes and retirement pens as if they were already dead." Then she asks rhetorically, a question implied by Butler in 1978: "Will this be the next liberation movement, another powerful ally in the new human politics by 1972 or 1976?"

The conversation with Butler no doubt caused Friedan to remember that experience with her mother in 1972. It also prompted her to do some initial research on aging. In 1979, she was awarded a $60,000 grant from the Ford Foundation to fund her research at Columbia University on two topics: the aging process and the shifting responsibilities of husband and wife within the family structure. Despite these early efforts, for the most part, Friedan ignored this pending project on aging because she was preoccupied with her campaign on the ERA. But, as Friedan later admitted, she avoided the project because she, too, was getting older. When her friends threw a surprise party on her 60th birthday in 1981, as she writes in the preface of *The Fountain of Age*, she could have killed them all. "Their toasts seemed hostile, insisting as they did that I publicly acknowledge reaching sixty, pushing me out of life . . . professionally, politically, personally, sexually." She was depressed for weeks because she could not face turning 60.

Then, as she had done many times before, Friedan rebounded. She accepted her age and made her project on aging a priority. She was selected as a distinguished scholar at Harvard's Institute of Politics in 1982, which gave her access to all the university's resources on aging. In her research, she learned that only 5 percent of the population over 65 suffered from Alzheimer's, but most published research on aging focused on this disease as well as other maladies of deterioration and decline in the aging population. Moreover, in the Harvard Medical School, seminars and studies dealt with practices of nursing homes, and in the Theological School, seminars included "Funeral Services" and "Concepts of the Afterlife." In the 1980s, she also attended meetings of various gerontology associations. She discovered at one conference that 90 percent of the presentations were about nursing homes, decline, dementia, and dying.

Friedan then decided to look elsewhere—to discover what older men and women were doing, rather than how the medical community and media were treating their aging process. She interviewed men and women in retirement hotels, trailer communities, and the upscale community where her mother lived. To gain firsthand experience, Friedan, in 1984, signed up for

"Going Beyond—Intensive for Adults 55 +." She spent a couple of weeks in the North Carolina mountains white-water rafting, shooting rapids with drops of 12 feet or more, backpacking, and learning how to use a compass. In 1988, she went to the Pritikin Longevity Center in Miami Beach because it was one of the few programs in the 1980s that assumed there could be vitality in old age. In two weeks, she lost 10 pounds, lowered her cholesterol and blood pressure, and jogged daily for 45 minutes. As a visiting scholar at the Andrus Gerontology Center at the University of Southern California (1986–1993), Friedan tested her findings by teaching a seminar on the mystique of age as well as using the center to further her research.

The process of research and writing *The Fountain of Age* was a birthing process that took 10 years. Although motivated by this project, Friedan had the distractions of lecturing, teaching, traveling, and, as always, she fell into the trap of overresearching the book. In 1988, she had a different distraction—but one that made her book far more personal and meaningful. That year her mother died.

In the 1980s, Miriam, still living in Leisure World, had a couple of accidents, suffering a broken leg and hip. She made a remarkable recovery, learning to use a cane to keep herself independent. After these accidents, Miriam's doctor told her to quit running duplicate bridge games because the responsibility caused her too much stress. Betty, who then lived in Southern California while teaching at the University of Southern California (USC), believed this was a great mistake. By telling Miriam to resign, the doctor had taken away the very framework that sustained her life by giving it "viable structure." Thereafter, Miriam's capacity to manage the daily skills of taking care of herself diminished. She often skipped meals and let the bathtub overflow a couple of times. Soon after Miriam's 90th birthday, Betty, her brother Harry, and her sister Amy decided that their mother needed to be moved to a nursing home. Because each of them had too many commitments to allocate time to monitor their mother's well-being, Betty and her siblings decided to relocate their mother to Milwaukee where Harry's daughter, a psychotherapist, lived. Betty and Harry moved Miriam to Milwaukee in the early spring of 1988. A few weeks later, Betty returned to see her mother. It was the last time they would be together.

In this last visit, as Friedan later wrote, she finally could put her arms around her mother and actually mean it when she said, "I love you." Miriam responded, "I know you do, darling, and I love you too." She, too, meant it. After seeing her mother, Friedan returned to Los Angeles to meet her teaching commitments at the Andrus Gerontology Center at USC. A few days later, she received the call that her mother had died. Miriam had lived in the nursing home for only six weeks. She was buried in Peoria next to her first husband, Harry Goldstein, and, as her mother's first child, Betty spoke at the funeral service.

Over the years, Betty had gained a greater understanding and respect for her mother. She greatly admired her mother's courage and determination to live a full life up to the moment that her independence was taken away. When Friedan finished *The Fountain of Age* in 1992, she honored her mother and her father by writing: "This book is dedicated to the memory of my mother, Miriam, and my father, Harry, who made a larger life possible for me." Friedan also told her children to never put her in a nursing home, and they obeyed.

The Fountain of Age, published 30 years after *The Feminine Mystique*, put Friedan, at 72, back on the *New York Times* bestseller list—albeit only for six weeks. Reviews were good, and profits from the book paid for adding a master bedroom and bath to her home in Sag Harbor. However, the author of a book that argued for vitality after 60 almost did not live to realize her success and to expand her home. After she sent the manuscript of her fourth book to the publisher, Friedan was hospitalized with heart failure.

While on vacation in Yosemite National Park, located in the High Sierra Mountains of California, Friedan had difficulty breathing. She thought it was caused by her lifelong bouts with asthma, but after going to a medical clinic in Yosemite, she learned that her heart was surrounded by fluid. She quickly returned to Los Angeles, made an appointment with a cardiologist, who told her that she had an infection in her aortic valve and was approaching heart failure. Friedan was taken by ambulance to the Good Samaritan Hospital, and her daughter Emily, a pediatrician, and her husband, a cardiologist, came to Los Angeles to assure that she had the best medical care possible. Friedan underwent open heart surgery to replace the infected valve.

Within months, the replacement valve failed and needed to be replaced. By the time of the second heart surgery, the publication date for *The Fountain of Age* was near, and Friedan was determined to promote her book. Among the first opportunities was the convention of the American Booksellers Association in Miami. She insisted on traveling to this convention, despite her daughter's protests. Friedan attended the convention, although she was confined to a wheelchair. Emily went along, just in case she, as a daughter and a doctor, might be needed. The second surgery in 1993 led to a complete recovery, one that lasted until 1997. That year Friedan had another heart valve replacement.

While working on *The Fountain of Age,* Betty Friedan also continued to pursue her concept that the family would serve as the new feminist frontier, which she had introduced in *The Second Stage.* She knew that the "real cutting edge of change" required new definitions of gender roles, structures of home and the workplace, and public policies that would allow "women to *choose* to have a family, with the knowledge that they will be able to retain their jobs if they opt for children and that there will be adequate day-care available." To advance her research, Friedan successfully applied for a one-year fellowship in 1994 at the Woodrow Wilson International Center for Scholars and was able to extend this award for a second year. To help facilitate her work, she gave up her apartment in New York City and moved to Washington, D.C.

At the Wilson Center, Friedan had the opportunity to consider and explore changing gender roles and public policy by organizing symposia on women, men, work, family, and public policy. Friedan and Heidi Hartmann, founder of the Institute for Women's Policy Research, co-chaired these meetings. They brought together leading experts from labor, corporations, Congress, and public policy agencies to examine the need for different models for the workplace and the family that reflected the changing economic and social realities of the 1990s. Entitled "The New Paradigm," this series of meetings challenged attendees to address current conflicts. Among the discussed topics were the upsurge of "angry white men" in the epidemic of corporate downsizing and dropping incomes, the bitter scapegoat of women and minorities as the foundation of a new backlash, the overload of work on the smaller workforce, and the stress caused by the loss of family time. Friedan used the narratives from the seminars as a basis for her fifth book, *Beyond Gender: The Real Politics of Work and Family*, published by Johns Hopkins University Press in 1997. She also used her work at the Wilson Center and her book as the basis for applying for continued funding for her research.

Encouraged by Susan Berresford, president of the Ford Foundation, Betty Friedan submitted a proposal to the Ford Foundation in 1998, requesting funding that would continue to support research and seminars on a "new paradigm" for working families and public policy. In response to her application, the Ford Foundation awarded Friedan a one million dollar grant to fund a four-year project. The requirements of the grant required the sponsorship of an academic institution. Friedan considered various universities but decided that Cornell University would be the best fit for the project. Cornell's advantages were that it already had established the Institute for Women and Work in its Industrial and Labor Relations with an extension division program in New York City.

Labeled "The New Paradigm Project: Women, Men, Work, Family, and Public Policy," Friedan, as a distinguished visiting professor at Cornell, organized a series of working conferences and roundtable strategy sessions to address crucial matters. The New Paradigm Project studied three central issues: (1) the restructured workplace and its impact on working families from low- to mid-level income occupations, (2) the need for corporate social responsibility and labor law reform in an age of international competition, and (3) the need for legislative initiatives on child care and universal health care. Within the context of these three issues, participants from traditionally polarized groups with ethnic, racial, national, and gender differences identified and examined the common concerns that were more pressing than those facing middle- and upper-middle-class families.

Between September 1998 and March 2000, Friedan served as a panelist on six of the nine seminars. Most topics reflected her vision of the "new frontier of feminism," and this was most certainly true when she was a panelist. For example, the first seminar returned to one of Friedan's key issues. Entitled "America's Obsession with Sex," the forum explored the current debate and media coverage of sexual politics in the American workplace and on Capitol Hill. In the December 1999 seminar, "Unlocking the Closed Door Policy of U.S. Child Care," the group explored an issue that Friedan had first identified in NOW's Bill of Rights for Women. Most likely shaped and driven by Friedan, the points of the discussion addressed the impact of the ongoing resistance of policy makers, business representatives, and unionists to universal child care and women's advancement in the workplace. In March 2000, Friedan moderated the discussion on "The Changing Nature of Work and Family Life: A Focus on Men." In this seminar participants were asked to address the following statement: "Since the 1960s, some feminists have argued that true gender equality will only be achieved when men fully share responsibilities at home." Clearly, such a topic and focus came directly from the lexicon of issues consistently posed by Betty Friedan.

Betty Friedan's work in The New Paradigm Project was not her only professional interest in the late 1990s. Pressured by family, friends, and colleagues, she also began working on her autobiography, a memoir of her "life so far." At first, Friedan resisted their suggestions. First, she believed that writing a memoir typically signals an end of a person's public life—and she was still going strong. Second, she wanted to expend her energy and time on finding new causes and projects, rather than looking backward on her lifetime of some seven decades. But she finally began to see that writing her autobiography had public and personal value.

Friedan initially decided to write her autobiography in order to "set the record straight." In the mid-1990s, she had been contacted and interviewed by two "self-appointed" biographers, whose interests and questions seemed to be peripheral to her life and work. She wanted to counter their conclusions, which she believed to be biased or just plain wrong. In addition, Friedan, like other public figures, realized that the approaching end of the twentieth century created public interest in how she had made significant contributions. As the millennium approached, *The Feminine Mystique* was listed as one of the one hundred most influential books written in the twentieth century. Thus Friedan felt compelled to use her memoir to reveal the personal story about the process of writing the book, and, more importantly, to tell others how she helped start the second-wave feminist movement that, in her view, changed the face of American history.

Her personal memoir, *Life So Far*, was published in 2000. Those familiar with Friedan's other books, also highly autobiographical, find much of the memoir repetitive. However, like all autobiographies, her memoir has the more important quality of revealing how she, as an individual and as a public figure, wanted to be remembered. As a public force, Friedan states that she never set out to "start a women's revolution." Rather "it just happened . . . by some miracle of convergence of family life and history, serendipity, one thing leading to another." Yet, at the same time, Friedan makes clear that once the women's movement began, she considered herself one of its most insightful, consistent, and faithful leaders.

Betty Friedan also makes clear that her approach to shaping, organizing, and promoting this unfinished revolution for women came from her own personal truth—that her public actions directly connected to experiences in her personal life. Said simply, the phrase, "the personal is political" was, for Friedan, a symbiotic relationship that engendered her lifelong quest to be an individual who is self-aware, honest, and stood by her convictions, which, in turn, empowered her public advocacy for equality and equity of women.

In the final chapter of *Life So Far*, Friedan connects her private and public lives when she reveals the underlying reason why she had spent some 50 years advocating women's rights. "I did it for my father," she writes, "so that men would not have the burden of their wives' frustration at having to live through them." Then she continues, "I did it for my mother, so that women would no longer have the discontent of dependency on their husbands, with no careers of their own." And finally, Friedan states that she "did it for my children, so that children would not have the burden of the mothers having to live through them."

Friedan concludes her memoir asserting that she was not ready to give up her public life. She was ready for new adventures. She would not be sidelined by being told to stay home and sit in a rocking chair. Then, Friedan looks back on her years with a great sense of satisfaction:

> In retrospect, I think how lucky I am that my life should have converged on history the way it did. The adventure of being able to use my life to transform society in a way none of us then would have ever dreamed possible is gratifying beyond measure. Whatever experiences I've had in my life—my education that I never thought I used in a real career, my mother's frustration which I finally understood, my learning experiences as a journalist in the labor movement, getting fired for pregnancy, freelancing for women's magazines in the "happy housewife" era, doing early voter research, plumbing the economic as well as the psychological underbelly of American life, the lasting joys as well as the regrets of my marriage, my aging—all of this I've used finally: I used it all. Who knows how I'll use it next?

Betty Friedan died on February 4, 2006—her 85th birthday. Because she had too few years to answer her own question, "Who knows what I will do next?" Friedan leaves behind this question for others to answer. It is the question that challenges women and men today to think about how their lives are both personal and political.

National Organization for Women

Statement of Purpose (1966)*

We, men and women who hereby constitute ourselves as the National Organization for Women, believe that the time has come for a new movement toward true equality for all women in America, and toward a fully equal partnership of the sexes, as part of the world-wide revolution of human rights now taking place within and beyond our national borders.

The purpose of NOW is to take action to bring women into full participation in the mainstream of American society now, exercising all the privileges and responsibilities thereof in truly equal partnership with men.

We believe the time has come to move beyond the abstract argument, discussion and symposia over the status and special nature of women which has raged in America in recent years; the time has come to confront, with concrete action, the conditions that now prevent women from enjoying the equality of opportunity and freedom of choice which is their right, as individual Americans, and as human beings.

---

*Note: This historic document was adopted at NOW's first national conference in Washington, D.C., on October 29, 1966. This Statement of Purpose was written by Betty Friedan.

NOW is dedicated to the proposition that women, first and foremost, are human beings, who, like all other people in our society, must have the chance to develop their fullest human potential. We believe that women can achieve such equality only by accepting to the full the challenges and responsibilities they share with all other people in our society, as part of the decision-making mainstream of American political, economic and social life.

We organize to initiate or support action, nationally, or in any part of this nation, by individuals or organizations, to break through the silken curtain of prejudice and discrimination against women in government, industry, the professions, the churches, the political parties, the judiciary, the labor unions, in education, science, medicine, law, religion and every other field of importance in American society.

Enormous changes taking place in our society make it both possible and urgently necessary to advance the unfinished revolution of women toward true equality, now. With a life span lengthened to nearly 75 years it is no longer either necessary or possible for women to devote the greater part of their lives to child-rearing; yet childbearing and rearing which continues to be a most important part of most women's lives—still is used to justify barring women from equal professional and economic participation and advance.

Today's technology has reduced most of the productive chores which women once performed in the home and in mass-production industries based upon routine unskilled labor. This same technology has virtually eliminated the quality of muscular strength as a criterion for filling most jobs, while intensifying American industry's need for creative intelligence. In view of this new industrial revolution created by automation in the mid-twentieth century, women can and must participate in old and new fields of society in full equality—or become permanent outsiders.

Despite all the talk about the status of American women in recent years, the actual position of women in the United States has declined, and is declining, to an alarming degree throughout the 1950's and 60's. Although 46.4% of all American women between the ages of 18 and 65 now work outside the home, the overwhelming majority—75%—are in routine clerical, sales, or factory jobs, or they are household workers, cleaning women, hospital attendants. About two-thirds of Negro women workers are in the lowest paid service occupations. Working women are becoming increasingly—not less—concentrated on the bottom of the job ladder. As a consequence full-time women workers today earn on the average only 60% of what men earn, and that wage gap has been increasing over the past twenty-five years in every major industry group. In 1964, of all women with a yearly income, 89% earned under $5,000 a year; half of all full-time year round women workers earned less than $3,690; only 1.4% of full-time year round women workers had an annual income of $10,000 or more.

Further, with higher education increasingly essential in today's society, too few women are entering and finishing college or going on to graduate or professional school. Today, women earn only one in three of the B.A.'s and M.A.'s granted, and one in ten of the Ph.D.'s.

In all the professions considered of importance to society, and in the executive ranks of industry and government, women are losing ground. Where they are present it is only a token handful. Women comprise less than 1% of federal judges; less than 4% of all lawyers; 7% of doctors. Yet women represent 51% of the U.S. population. And, increasingly, men are replacing women in the top positions in secondary and elementary schools, in social work, and in libraries—once thought to be women's fields.

Official pronouncements of the advance in the status of women hide not only the reality of this dangerous decline, but the fact that nothing is being done to stop it. The excellent reports of the President's Commission on the Status of Women and of the State Commissions have not been fully implemented. Such Commissions have power only to advise. They have no power to enforce their recommendation; nor have they the freedom to organize American women and men to press for action on them. The reports of these commissions have, however, created a basis upon which it is now possible to build. Discrimination in employment on the basis of sex is now prohibited by federal law, in Title VII of the Civil Rights Act of 1964. But although nearly one-third of the cases brought before the Equal Employment Opportunity Commission during the first year dealt with sex discrimination and the proportion is increasing dramatically, the Commis-sion has not made clear its intention to enforce the law with the same seriousness on behalf of women as of other victims of discrimination. Many of these cases were Negro women, who are the victims of double discrimination of race and sex. Until now, too few women's organizations and official spokesmen have been willing to speak out against these dangers facing women. Too many women have been restrained by the fear of being called "feminist." There is no civil rights movement to speak for women, as there has been for Negroes and other victims of discrimination. The National Organization for Women must therefore begin to speak.

WE BELIEVE that the power of American law, and the protection guaranteed by the U.S. Constitution to the civil rights of all individuals, must be effectively applied and enforced to isolate and remove patterns of sex discrimination, to ensure equality of opportunity in employment and education, and equality of civil and political rights and responsibilities on behalf of women, as well as for Negroes and other deprived groups.

We realize that women's problems are linked to many broader questions of social justice; their solution will require concerted action by many groups. Therefore, convinced that human rights for all are indivisible, we expect to give active support to the common cause of equal rights for all those who suffer discrimination and deprivation, and we call upon other organizations committed to such goals to support our efforts toward equality for women.

WE DO NOT ACCEPT the token appointment of a few women to high-level positions in government and industry as a substitute for serious continuing effort to recruit and advance women according to their individual abilities. To this end, we urge American government and industry to mobilize the same resources of ingenuity and command with which they have solved problems of far greater difficulty than those now impeding the progress of women.

WE BELIEVE that this nation has a capacity at least as great as other nations, to innovate new social institutions which will enable women to enjoy the true equality of opportunity and responsibility in society, without conflict with their responsibilities as mothers and homemakers. In such innovations, America does not lead the Western world, but lags by decades behind many European countries. We do not accept the traditional assumption that a woman has to choose between marriage and motherhood, on the one hand, and serious participation in industry or the professions on the other. We question the present expectation that all normal women will retire from job or profession for 10 or 15 years, to devote their full time to raising children, only to reenter the job market at a relatively minor level. This, in itself, is a deterrent to the aspirations of women, to their acceptance into management or professional training courses, and to the very possibility of equality of opportunity or real choice, for all but a few women. Above all, we reject the assumption that these problems are the unique responsibility of each individual woman, rather than a basic social dilemma which society must solve. True equality of opportunity and freedom of choice for women requires such practical and possible innovations as a nationwide network of child-care centers, which will make it unnecessary for women to retire completely from society until their children are grown, and national programs to provide retraining for women who have chosen to care for their children full-time.

WE BELIEVE that it is as essential for every girl to be educated to her full potential of human ability as it is for every boy—with the knowledge that such education is the key to effective participation in today's economy and that, for a girl as for a boy, education can only be serious where there is expectation that it will be used in society. We believe that American educators are capable of devising means of imparting such expectations to girl students. Moreover, we consider the decline in the proportion of women receiving higher and professional education to be evidence of discrimination. This discrimination may take the form of quotas against the admission of women to colleges, and professional schools; lack of encouragement by parents, counselors and educators; denial of loans or fellowships; or the traditional or arbitrary procedures in graduate and professional training geared in terms of men, which inadvertently discriminate against women. We believe that the same serious attention must be given to high school dropouts who are girls as to boys.

WE REJECT the current assumptions that a man must carry the sole burden of supporting himself, his wife, and family, and that a woman is automatically entitled to lifelong support by a man upon her marriage, or that marriage, home and family are primarily woman's world and responsibility—hers, to dominate— his to support. We believe that a true partnership between the sexes demands a different concept of marriage, an equitable sharing of the responsibilities of home and children and of the economic burdens of their support. We believe that proper recognition should be given to the economic and social value of homemaking and child-care. To these ends, we will seek to open a reexamination of laws and mores governing marriage and divorce, for we believe that the current state of "half-equity" between the sexes discriminates against both men and women, and is the cause of much unnecessary hostility between the sexes.

WE BELIEVE that women must now exercise their political rights and responsibilities as American citizens. They must refuse to be segregated on the basis of sex into separate-and-not-equal ladies' auxiliaries in the political parties, and they must demand representation according to their numbers in the regularly constituted party committees—at local, state, and national levels—and in the informal power structure, participating fully in the selection of candidates and political decision-making, and running for office themselves.

IN THE INTERESTS OF THE HUMAN DIGNITY OF WOMEN, we will protest, and endeavor to change, the false image of women now prevalent in the mass media, and in the texts, ceremonies, laws, and practices of our major social institutions. Such images perpetuate contempt for women by society and by women for themselves. We are similarly opposed to all policies and practices—in church, state, college, factory, or office—which, in the guise of protectiveness, not only deny opportunities but also foster in women self-denigration, dependence, and evasion of responsibility, undermine their confidence in their own abilities and foster contempt for women.

NOW WILL HOLD ITSELF INDEPENDENT OF ANY POLITI- CAL PARTY in order to mobilize the political power of all women and men intent on our goals. We will strive to ensure that no party, candidate, president, senator, governor, congressman, or any public official who betrays or ignores the principle of full equality between the sexes is elected or appointed to office. If it is necessary to mobilize the votes of men and women who believe in our cause, in order to win for women the final right to be fully free and equal human beings, we so commit ourselves.

WE BELIEVE THAT women will do most to create a new image of women by acting now, and by speaking out in behalf of their own equality, freedom, and human dignity—not in pleas for special privilege, nor in enmity toward men, who are also victims of the current, half-equality between the sexes—but in an active, self-respecting partnership with men. By so doing, women will develop confidence in their own ability to determine actively, in partnership with men, the conditions of their life, their choices, their future and their society.

National Organization for Women

Bill of Rights for Women (1968)*

I. Equal Rights Constitutional Amendment
II. Enforce Law Banning Sex Discrimination in Employment
III. Maternity Leave Rights in Employment and in Social Security Benefits
IV. Tax Deduction for Home and Child Care Expenses for Working Parents
V. Child Day Care Centers
VI. Equal and Unsegregated Education
VII. Equal Job Training Opportunities and Allowances for Women in Poverty
VIII. The Right of Women to Control Their Reproductive Lives

We demand

I. That the United States Congress immediately pass the Equal Rights Amendment to the Constitution to provide that "Equality of rights under the law shall not be denied or abridged by the United States or by any State on account of sex" and that such then be immediately ratified by the several States.

---

*Adopted at the 1967 National Conference of NOW. Written by Betty Friedan.

II. That equal employment opportunity be guaranteed to all women, as well as men, by insisting that the Equal Employment Opportunity Commission enforce the prohibitions against sex discrimination in employment under Title VII of the Civil Rights Act of 1964 with the same vigor as it enforces the prohibitions against racial discrimination.

III. That women be protected by law to insure their rights to return to their jobs within a reasonable time after childbirth without loss of seniority or other accrued benefits and be paid maternity leave as a form of social security and/or employee benefit.

IV. Immediate revision of tax laws to permit the deduction of home and child care expenses for working parents.

V. That child care facilities be established by law on the same basis as parks, libraries and public schools adequate to the needs of children, from the pre-school years through adolescence, as a community resource to be used by all citizens from all income levels.

VI. That the right of women to be educated to their full potential equally with men be secured by Federal and State legislation, eliminating all discrimination and segregation by sex, written and unwritten, at all levels of education including college, graduate and professional schools, loans and fellowships and Federal and State training programs, such as the Job Corps.

VII. The right of women in poverty to secure job training, housing and family allowances on equal terms with men, but without prejudice to a parent's right to remain at home to care for his or her children; revision of welfare legislation and poverty programs which deny women dignity, privacy and self respect.

VIII. The right of women to control their own reproductive lives by removing from penal codes the laws limiting access to contraceptive information and devices and laws governing abortion.

Study and Discussion Questions

Chapter 1: Through a Glass Darkly

1. Compare and contrast Bettye's relationship and interactions with her mother and with her father. How did she receive positive reinforcement from each parent? What were some of the negative aspects of her relationship with each of them? Provide specific examples.

2. Starting with first grade, school became a positive force in Bettye's life because learning, extracurricular activities, and friendships increased her self-confidence. Identify and describe two examples of how school served as a positive force. Select at least one example from her high school years.

3. As an adult, Friedan often referred to her experiences of not being asked to join a sorority in high school. Why did she think she was rejected? How did her parents counsel her? How did this experience change her attitude about herself? Why do you think she cited this experience so often once she had become a leader in the women's movement?

4. In her high school autobiography, "Through a Glass Darkly," Bettye wrote that her long-term goal was to "fall in love and be loved and be needed by someone" and "to have children." And she wanted something more: "I want to do something with my life—to have an absorbing interest. I want success and fame." What factors in her family life and her observations about her mother might have caused her to make this statement?

Chapter 2: Exploring the Life of the Mind

1. Describe Smith College—its location, size, student population, and learning and living environments. For Bettye, in what ways would attending Smith College been similar to living in Peoria, Illinois? How would it be different?

2. During her first semester at Smith College, Bettye confronted her Jewish identity. How did this experience increase her self-confidence and awaken her political awareness?

3. Describe how courses with James Gibson and Dorothy Wolff Douglas were especially significant to her learning experience. In what ways do you think these courses were factors in shaping Friedan's advocacy for women's rights?

4. In *Life So Far*, Friedan writes that the lasting significance of her education at Smith College was that she had gained from Smith an "inescapable social conscience" and "an inescapable sense of political responsibility." In what ways did she act on this responsibility in her final two years at Smith College? Describe two or three examples from her actions as editor of SCAN and SCM and/or her summer internship at Highlander Folk School.

Chapter 3: Working for the Revolution

1. How did working at *Federated Press* (FP) meet Betty's objective to "work for the revolution"? What was the political stance of *FP,* and who were its subscribers? Whose rights did it promote, and why was it critical of the policies of the Roosevelt administration in the 1940s?

2. At *FP,* Betty focused on issues facing women as workers, housewives, and consumers. How did she address these issues in "Pretty Posters Won't Stop Turnover of Women in Industry"? Provide two specific examples from the contents of this article, paying particular attention to the interview with Ruth Young.

3. "UE Fights for Women Workers" represents Betty's strongest argument for women workers. What examples do you find

to be most persuasive? Review the list of demands in "UE's Program For Women." Are there any points that would be relevant to a women's rights movement? Are there any points that are still relevant today?

4. In 1974, Friedan wrote "The Way We Were—1949" for *New York* magazine. In part, she states, as a radical, she was not concerned about the rights of women. Rather, she, along with other radicals, was only concerned about the rights of Negroes and the working class and about the corrosive impact of McCarthyism and the House Un-American Activities Committee. Based on the information in this chapter about her articles for *FP* and *UE News*, do you think Friedan made an accurate statement in 1974? Why or why not? Provide specific examples.

Chapter 4: Homeward Bound

1. As a high school senior, Betty had decided she wanted to be married, have children, and have an "absorbing interest" outside the home that brought her "success and fame." How did she achieve these objectives in the late 1940s and early 1950s? What challenges did she face when she tried to combine her role as a wife and mother and her decision to have a career as a freelance writer?

2. In 1974, Friedan wrote that "the concrete, palatable actuality of the carpentry and the cooking you could do yourself and the surprising effectiveness of the changes you could make happen in school boards and zoning and community politics, were somehow more real and secure than the schizophrenic and even dangerous politics of the world revolution." In sum, suburbia and children served as the "comfortable small world" that she, like other women like her, "could really do something about, politically." Although specific to the concerns of the Cold War, this statement implies that a woman, as a wife and mother, has more influence at home than in the public sphere. Do you agree? Why or why not?

3. In what ways was Friedan not a typical suburban housewife who lived in Rockland County? Consider her work as a

freelance writer and as a founder and director of the Intellectual Resources Pool.

Chapter 5: Defrocking the Myth

1. The theories presented by Maryina Farnham and Ferdinand Lundberg in *Modern Woman: The Lost Sex* and by Adlai Stevenson in his "Commencement Address at Smith College" in 1955 were fundamental to Friedan's decisions about questions to include on the "Smith College Anonymous Questionnaire for the Fifteen-Year Reunion." What were the central ideas presented by Farnham and Lundberg in *Modern Woman*? How did Stevenson define the role of college-educated women in the 1950s? What was Friedan's opinion about each of these?

2. Describe Friedan's research process for *The Feminine Mystique*. What were her sources of information? Describe and evaluate the value of at least three categories of her research (e.g., interviews, women's magazines, etc.).

3. What is Friedan's central argument in *The Feminine Mystique*? How does she defrock the "modern woman" from her cultural wrappings of the feminine mystique?

4. In the last two chapters of *The Feminine Mystique*, Friedan offers some solutions. How feasible is Friedan's "New Life Plan for Women" for a young woman living in suburbia who had two or three small children? What kind of support systems would she need to engage in Friedan's New Life Plan?

5. Although critics argue that *The Feminine Mystique* is limited to the experiences of white middle-class women living in suburbia, Friedan's book was a key factor that led to the second-wave feminist movement and inspired many to become feminist activists. What are some of the reasons cited in the chapter that account for the book's impact? For example, would Friedan's "New Life Plan for Women" have appealed to working-class women and women of color? Is Friedan's plan relevant and/or still needed today?

Chapter 6: Reluctant Heroines

1. In mid-1963, Friedan signed a book contract with Random House and in 1964, she had the chance to showcase her research in the *Ladies' Home Journal*. What does Friedan mean by the "fourth dimension"? How does it demonstrate that women had moved beyond the feminine mystique? Does Friedan's concept of the fourth dimension have any similarities to the New Life Plan she presents in *The Feminine Mystique*? If so, what are these similarities?

2. Describe the three groups of women that comprised the second wave of feminism. Be clear about the demographic characteristics and political vantage point of each group.

3. Explain the significance of Title VII of the Civil Rights Act of 1964 for women's rights. How did the Equal Employment Opportunity Commission (EEOC) react to the provision to assure an end to sex discrimination in the workplace?

4. In NOW's "Statement of Purpose" (see Appendix A), Friedan articulates her concept of feminism. What is this concept? In what ways is the Statement of Purpose inclusive of working-class women and women of color and of the assertion that women's rights are human rights? What culturally defined group of women is missing in this document?

5. Friedan claimed in 1976 that she and others who organized NOW in 1966 were "reluctant heroines" who "identified, as women, with Everywoman." Do you think Friedan was a reluctant heroine? Cite specific examples that support your opinion.

Chapter 7: The Unfinished Revolution

1. In the summer of 1966, Friedan decided to make sex discrimination in the workplace the one-issue agenda of NOW. What were the four areas of NOW's offensives? What were the outcomes of NOW's actions?

2. What are the demands of NOW's Bill of Rights for Women (see Appendix B)? Why were the demands that women have

access to legal abortion and the ratification of the Equal Rights Amendment considered the "most revolutionary" demands in the late 1960s? Are these demands still considered as revolutionary today?

3. How did feminists in the women's liberation movement define sexual politics? Why did they believe a process of consciousness-raising was the essential first step of a woman's liberation? Why did Friedan disagree with the claims made by the women's liberation groups and their method of consciousness-raising?

4. Friedan decided to oppose public support for the lesbian rights because she feared that NOW would be perceived as "anti-male." What were the three areas of potential fall-out? What actions did Friedan take that offended lesbians in NOW? How did her actions damage her ability to sustain her role as NOW's president?

5. The Women's Strike for Equality is a high point of the women's movement and its success is directly attributable to Friedan. Select one or two examples that illustrate how she made this event successful.

6. How did Friedan, as president, assure the success of NOW in its early and most fragile years? Identify and describe two or three examples that are discussed in the final pages of Chapter 7.

Chapter 8: Transcending Polarities

1. By the early 1970s, Friedan had been sidelined by feminists in NOW and the women's liberation movement. In response, she decided to use her writing, her travel to foreign countries, her membership in other organizations, and her invitations to teach as new venues to promote and test her ideas. Select two examples and describe Friedan's actions. In your opinion, were her efforts successful? Why or why not? Be specific.

2. Evaluate the ways that Friedan lobbied for a woman's right to a legal abortion from 1968 to 1973. In her comments at

the first meeting of the NARAL, how did she connect a woman's right to choose and a person's inalienable right to personal liberty? How did *Roe v. Wade* immediately affect the lives of women?

3. Much to Friedan's credit, the U.S. Congress approved the Equal Rights Amendment in 1972, and by 1973, 30 states had ratified it. Yet the ERA had significant opposition from Phyllis Schlafly. Evaluate the assumptions and actions of Schlafly about women's rights and women's role in American society. Why did Schlafly oppose feminism? Who were her supporters? In what ways did she attack NOW?

Chapter 9: New Feminist Frontiers

1. Explain the motivation, organization, and selection of delegates to the National Women's Conference. What were the issues listed in the 26 resolutions of the National Plan of Action? Did these resolutions reflect some of Friedan's ideas for women's full equality with men? Which three resolutions were the most controversial and why?

2. What is the significance of Friedan's statement about the lesbian rights resolution? How did lesbians and their supporters react to Friedan's statement and the vote that followed? How did Schlafly and her supporters react to the vote and demonstration?

3. In *The Second Stage*, Friedan presented the family as the "new feminist frontier." What are her assumptions and her argument? How is Friedan's concept of a new feminist frontier consistent with her assumptions and solutions in *The Feminine Mystique*, NOW's Statement of Purpose, and the Women's Bill of Rights?

4. In part, Friedan decided to write *The Fountain of Age* because she believed a study on aging would be another dimension of a woman's right to full equality. Why did she make that assumption? What was the connection between her research on aging and her relationship with her mother in the 1970s and 1980s?

5. Friedan continued to pursue her interest in the family as the new feminist frontier at the Woodrow Wilson International Center for Scholars and in The New Paradigm Project. In what ways do each of these projects correspond to her previous writings and her feminist ideas? How relevant are the issues discussed within each of these projects today?

6. Friedan died on February 4, 2006. In your opinion, what are her greatest contributions to women's rights, to second-wave feminism, and to the issues of third-wave feminism?

A Note on the Sources

The Writings of Betty Friedan

Any study on Betty Friedan begins with her published writings. Friedan authored five books, and each addresses specific problems faced by women and proposes solutions. The themes and interpretations are shaped by Friedan's experiences and attitudes. Thus these works serve a not only as a running history of the issues and actions of the second-wave feminist movement and the conservative backlash that followed but also as an autobiographical commentary. As we consider the entirety of her writing, we realize that Friedan is consistent: She believed women were treated unequally by men and by society, and she argued that to end this second-tier status would require changes in public policies and legislation and a partnership as equals with men. Friedan first made this argument in *The Feminine Mystique* (New York: W.W. Norton & Company, Inc., 1963), which still stands as her best known and most important contribution to the modern women's movement. She continues with this interpretation in *It Changed My Life* (New York: Random House, 1976), where she tells "herstory" of the tumultuous years of the women's movement. In her next two books, *The Second Stage* (New York: Summit Books, 1981) and *Beyond Gender: The New Politics of Work and Family* (Washington, D.C.: Woodrow Wilson Center Press, 1997), Friedan responds to the postfeminist era by arguing that the family is the "new feminist frontier." In both books, Friedan harkens back to the consistent theme that true equality requires that men and women share equally the responsibilities in the home and in the need to generate income, and that "to make this so" requires "family-friendly" support systems such as publicly funded child care. In *The Fountain of Age* (New York: Simon & Schuster, 1993), Friedan expands her demand for true equality by making the case that society should not marginalize people over age 65. Her book was one of the first of many to make this argument. *Life So Far* (New York: Simon & Schuster, 2000) is Friedan's autobiography. Although it repeats much of what she wrote in her earlier books, it is valuable for revealing what Friedan believed to be significant about her life.

Friedan's personal and public papers are located at the Arthur and Elizabeth Schlesinger Library on the History of Women in America. For this biography, access to these papers has been instrumental. For example, as a high school senior, Friedan wrote her autobiography for an English assignment. Entitled "Through a Glass Darkly," the autobiography provides insights into how she viewed herself, her mother and father, and her friends at age 17. Such documentation, essential to any analysis of her early years, was used in this book.

Likewise, the Friedan papers include copies of her published and unpublished writings at Smith College. Those used in this work include "Learning the Score, We Know the Score" and "Work and Write—a Highlander Project," both written when Friedan was part of the summer internship program at Highlander Folk School. Another example is "The Scapegoat," a fictionalized account of Friedan's struggle with her Jewish identity during her first year at Smith College. Although not used in this biography, it is an important source.

Finally, Friedan's personal papers provide additional insights into her process of writing *The Feminine Mystique*. Twenty of the 200 questionnaires from "Smith 1942—Fifteen Years Later" are available on microfilm, and in reading these, it's clear that they comprise the heart of Friedan's conclusions. More significantly, Friedan's completed questionnaire is available, and her responses help us understand her attitudes, economic struggles, and concerns as a wife and mother in 1957. In addition, the Friedan papers include numerous drafts of an article she wanted to publish about the findings of the Smith survey. By reading these, as well as the various drafts of *The Feminine Mystique*, Friedan's thought processes as she wrote the book are revealed. Equally significant is the letter that Gerda Lerner sent to Friedan on February 6, 1963, in which, as noted in this biography, Lerner skillfully notes the strengths and shortcomings of Friedan's analysis in *The Feminine Mystique*.

As a public figure, Friedan wrote numerous articles. Her articles for the *Federated Press* are located at The Rare Books and Manuscript Collection at Columbia University, and her published work for *UE News* can be acquired from the UE archives in Pittsburgh, Pennsylvania, at the United Electrical Radio & Machine Workers of America.

Biographies and Biographical Profiles of Betty Friedan

The two major biographies of Friedan are *Betty Friedan and the Making of The Feminine Mystique* (Amherst: University of Massachusetts Press, 1998) by Daniel Horowitz and *Betty Friedan: Her Life* (New York: Random House, 1999) by Judith Hennessee. Neither were "authorized biographies," and Friedan claimed that both authors had "gotten it all wrong."

Nonetheless, Horowitz and Hennessee make significant contributions in their respective works. Horowitz, a cultural historian, argues persuasively that Friedan's feminism was rooted not only in the suburban captivity of the 1950s, as she claimed, but also in the labor radicalism of the 1940s. To make his case, Horowitz focuses attention on Friedan's life prior to the publication of *The Feminine Mystique*. In part, he relies on the work of Rachel Bowlby, "The Problem with No Name Rereading Friedan's *The Feminine Mystique*," *Feminist Review* (September 1987); Susan Hartman, "Women's Employment and the Domestic Ideal in the Early Cold War Years," and Joanne Meyerowitz, "Beyond *The Feminine Mystique: A Reassessment of Postwar Mass Culture, 1946–1958*." The essays by Hartman and Meyerowitz are included in the latter's *Not June Cleaver: Women and Gender in Postwar America, 1945–1960* (Philadelphia: Temple University Press, 1994).

Judith Hennessee, a journalist, set out to write a definitive biography of Friedan, but her work does not match her objective.

The value of Hennessee's work is that she interviewed Friedan's family as well as her friends and enemies. But the shortcoming of the book as a source is that Hennessee provides details about battles but does not address the larger issues and the conflicts in the second-wave feminist movement objectively. Both biographies were useful sources for this book. Horowitz's work was most helpful when evaluating Friedan's years in college and as a labor journalist; Hennessee's work was useful to sort out the details of Friedan's personal life and her interactions with family, friends, and feminists.

Interviews with and profiles of Friedan are also rich with detail and insights. Often used in anthologies and academic readers are Marcia Cohen's "If They Don't Like Me" and "*The Feminine Mystique*," included in *The Sisterhood: The True Story of the Women Who Changed the World* (New York: Simon & Schuster, 1988). Another resource is Jacqueline Van Voris, *The Smith Centennial Study: Oral History Project: A Smith Mosaic* (Northampton: Smith College, 1975). The more expansive resource on Friedan is *Interviews with Betty Friedan* (Jackson: University Press of Mississippi, 2002). This collection of 22 interviews spans 36 years (1963 to 1999) and publications as diverse as the *New York Times, Working Woman,* and *Playboy*. Read sequentially, they provide a road map to Friedan's activism and travails. For this biography the most useful interviews were Marilyn French's "The Emancipation of Betty Friedan;" Lyn Tornabene's "The Liberation of Betty Friedan;" Mary Walton's "Once More to the Ramparts;" and Paul Wilkes's "Mother Superior to Women's Lib."

The Second Wave of Feminism

The literature about the second-wave feminist movement is robust and diverse. The sources listed here are selective and most relevant to Friedan's influence, issues, and impact.

General Histories

Friedan and the complexity of the second wave of feminism receives an objective, well-researched, and thoughtful analysis in William H. Chafe, *The Paradox of Change* (New York: Oxford

University Press, 1991); Ruth Rosen, *The World Split Open, How the Modern Women's Movement Changed America* (New York: Viking Penguin Putnam, Inc., 2000); and Shelia Tobias, *Faces of Feminism: An Activist's Reflections on the Women's Movement* (Boulder: Westview Press, 1997). As participants in the movement, Rosen and Tobias relied on their experiences of key events as well as on their network of feminists. Yet both present the issues and conflicts with objectivity and clarity. Nancy Woloch offers a critical evaluation of Friedan and an excellent synthesis of second-wave feminism in the latter chapters of *Women and the American Experience* (Boston: McGraw Hill, 2006). Elaine Tyler May's analysis of domestic containment in *Homeward Bound: American Families in the Cold War Era* (New York: Basic Books, 1999) has been incorporated in this biography as well.

Other significant works written by participants in the second-wave feminist movement include Flora Davis, *Moving the Mountain: The Women's Movement in America since 1960* (New York: Simon & Schuster, 1991); Sarah Evans, *Personal Politics: The Roots of Women's Liberation in the Civil Rights Movement and the New Left* (New York: Knopf, 1979), and *Tidal Wave: How Women Changed America at Century's End* (New York: Free Press, 2003); Estelle B. Freedman, *No Turning Back: The History of Feminism and the Future of Women* (New York: Ballantine Books, 2002); Jo Freeman, *The Women's Liberation Movement: Its Aims, Structures, and Ideas* (Pittsburgh: KNOW, Inc., 1971), and *The Politics of Women's Liberation: A Case Study of an Emerging Social Movement and Its Relationship to the Policy Process* (New York: Longman, 1975); Susan Hartman, *The Home Front and Beyond: American Women in the 1940s* (Boston: Twayne, 1982) and *From Margin to Mainstream: American Women and Politics since 1960* (New York: Alfred A. Knopf, 1989).

Topics Relevant to Betty Friedan

Like Friedan, other feminists have written memoirs of their activism. Those that make useful comparisons to Friedan's writings are Susan Brownmiller, *In Our Time* (New York: Dial Press, 1999); Gerda Lerner, *Fireweed: A Political Autobiography*

(Philadelphia: Temple University Press, 2002); and Gloria Steinem, *Outrageous Acts and Everyday Rebellions* (New York: Holt, Rinehart, and Winston, 1983). As an anthology of that time period, Robin Morgan's *Sisterhood Is Powerful* (New York: Vintage, 1970) must be read.

A definitive history of NOW has yet to be written. Frances Kolb, now deceased, initiated such a history, "The National Organization for Women: A History of the First Ten Years." Her unpublished manuscript and audiotape collection (1979–81) are located at the Arthur and Elizabeth Schlesinger Library on the History of Women in America. In the absence of an "official history" is Toni Carabillo's *The Feminist Chronicles, 1953–1993* (Los Angeles: Women's Graphics, 1993). This source is also available online. Carabillo's work has been helpful in this biography because it details the actions of NOW when Friedan served as its president.

Reading significant feminist tracts provides a context to understanding Friedan's opposition to sexual politics. Among the works that were widely read and debated during the second-wave feminist movement are Jessie Bernard, *The Future of Marriage* (New York: Bantam Books, 1978); Caroline Bird, *Born Female* (New York: Pocket Books, 1969); Shulamith Firestone, *The Dialectic of Sex: The Case for Feminist Revolution* (New York: Morrow, 1970); Germaine Greer, *The Female Eunuch* (New York: McGraw Hill, 1972); Kate Millett, *Sexual Politics* (New York: Avon, 1971); Jill Johnson, *Lesbian Nation: The Feminist Solution* (New York: Simon & Schuster, 1973); Ti-Grace Atkinson, *Amazon Odyssey* (New York: Links Books, 1974); Adrienne Rich, *Of Woman Born* (New York: W.W. Norton & Co., 1976); and Susan Brownmiller, *Against Our Will* (New York: Bantam Books, 1976).

It is equally important to understand the issues and politics of antifeminism, and the obvious place to begin is with Phyllis Schlafly's *The Power of the Positive Woman* (New York: Harcourt Brace Jovanovic, 1978). Two biographies also detail Schlafly's private and public life: Carol Felsenthal, *The Sweetheart of the Silent Majority: The Biography of Phyllis Schlafly* (Chicago: Doubleday & Co., 1981), and Donald Critchlow, *Phyllis Schlafly and Grassroots Conservatism* (Princeton: Princeton University

Press, 2005). Susan Faludi's *Backlash: The Undeclared War Against American Women* (New York: Anchor Books, 1991) examines the resurgence of antifeminism in the 1980s. In part, Faludi argues that Friedan had become almost antifeminist by the early 1980s, using *The Second Stage* as evidence. Relevant to the failure of ratification of the ERA, see Mary Frances Berry, *Why ERA Failed: Politics, Women's Rights, and the Amending Process of the Constitution* (Bloomington: Indiana University Press, 1986), and Jane J. Mansbridge, *Why We Lost the ERA* (Chicago: University of Chicago Press, 1986).

Primary Sources

Although not used for this biography, any study of Friedan would be incomplete without the primary sources and personal narratives of the second-wave feminist movement. Worthy of mention are Dawn Keetley and John Pettegrew, eds., *Public Women, Public Words: A Documentary History of American Feminism, vol. 3, 1960 to the Present* (Madison: Madison House, 2002); Rosayn Baxandall and Linda Gordon, eds., *Dear Sisters: Dispatches from the Women's Liberation Movement* (New York: Basic Books, 2000); Bonnie Watkins and Nina Rothchild, eds., *In the Company of Women: Voices from the Women's Movement* (Minneapolis: Minnesota Historical Society Press, 1998); and Rachel Blau DePlessix and Ann Snitow, eds., *The Feminist Memoir Project* (New York: Three Rivers Press, 1998). More recent is *The "Second Wave" and Beyond: Women and Social Movements Community*, a Web-based resource launched in 2006. The objectives of this resource are "to bring together feminist thinkers, scholars, and activists to analyze compelling questions about feminist activism and theories, define new directions for historical research on this period, and provide a new venue for publishing traditional articles but also for writing and recording this history in ways made possible by the medium of online publication." Its editors are Stephanie Gilmore, Judith Ezekiel, Kimberly Springer, and Sherri L. Barnes. The Web site is sponsored by Alexander Street Press (http://scholar.alexanderstreet. com).

Index